Think Python

A Beginner's Guide with Machine Programming Language, Including an Intensive Course with Step-By-Step Exercises to Learn Python Code in 7 Days

WILLIAMS PARK

TABLE OF CONTENTS

Introduction

Congratulations on downloading Think Python: *A beginner's guide with machine programming language, including an intensive course with step-by-step exercises to learn Python code in 7 days* and thank you for doing so.

The following chapters will discuss various fundamental concepts of the Python programming language and machine learning. There are 6 chapters in this book, crafted specifically to help you master basic and advanced python programming concepts required to develop web-based programs and applications in just a week.

The first chapter will provide you an introduction to machine learning and various terminologies that are frequently used in this field. You will understand the significance of machine learning in our daily lives. The second chapter of this book will provide a detailed overview of Python and its historical development. Step by step instructions to install Python on your operating systems have also been included. The concept of Python comments, variables and data types that serve as a prerequisite to the learning of Python programming have been explained in detail. The chapter 3 is a detailed overview of the basic concepts of Python programming focusing on various programming elements such as Booleans, Tuples, Sets, Dictionaries and much more. The chapter 4 pertains to the advance Python programming concepts that are relatively more complicated and require a solid understanding of the basic concepts. You will learn how to use OOPS concepts, different loops and conditional statements to generate sophisticated commands. The chapter 5 contains a list of all such built-in functions, methods and keywords that can be used to easily develop and run advance codes. The final chapter "Python Applications" will provide details on how Python programming is being used in development and testing of software programs, machine learning algorithms and Artificial Intelligence technologies to solve real world problems.

There are plenty of books on this subject on the market, thanks again for choosing this one! Every effort was made to ensure it is full of as much useful information as possible, please enjoy!

Chapter 1:

Introduction to Machine Learning

The modern concept of Artificial Intelligence technology is derived from the idea that machines are capable of human like intelligence and potentially mimic human thought processing and learning capabilities to adapt to fresh inputs and perform tasks with no human assistance. Machine learning is integral to the concept of artificial intelligence. Machine Learning can be defined as a concept of Artificial Intelligence technology that focuses primarily on the engineered capability of machines to explicitly learn and self-train, by identifying data patterns to improve upon the underlying algorithm and make independent decisions with no human intervention. In 1959, pioneering computer gaming and artificial intelligence expert, Arthur Samuel, coined the term "machine learning" during his tenure at IBM.

Machine learning stems from the hypothesis that modern day computers have an ability to be trained by utilizing targeted training data sets, that can be easily customized to develop desired functionalities. Machine learning is driven by the pattern recognition technique where in the machine records and revisits past interactions and results, that are deemed in alignment with its current situation. Given the fact that machines are required to process endless amount of data, with new data always pouring in, they must be equipped to adapt to the new data without needing to be programmed by a human, which speaks to the iterative aspect of machine learning.

Now the topic of machine learning is so "hot" that the world of academia, business as well as the scientific community have their own take on its definition. Here are a few of the widely accepted definitions from select highly reputed sources:

- *"Machine learning is the science of getting computers to act without being explicitly programmed."* – Stanford University

- *"The field of Machine Learning seeks to answer the question - How can we build computer systems that automatically improve with experience, and what are the fundamental laws that govern all learning processes?"* – Carnegie Mellon University

- *"Machine learning algorithms can figure out how to perform important tasks by generalizing from examples."* – University of Washington

- *"Machine Learning at its most basic is the practice of using algorithms to parse data, learn from it, and then make a determination or prediction about something in the world."* – Nvidia

- *"Machine learning is based on algorithms that can learn from data without relying on rules-based programming."* – McKinsey & Co.

Core Concepts of Machine Learning

The biggest draw of this technology is its inherent ability allowing the system to automatically learn programs from the raw data in lieu of manually engineering the program for the machine. Over the last ten years or so the application of ML algorithms has expanded from computer science labs to the industrial world. Machine learning algorithms are capable of generalizing tasks so they can be executed iteratively. The process of developing specific programs for specific tasks is extremely taxing in terms of time and money but occasionally it is just impossible to achieve. On the other hand, machine learning programming is often feasible and tends to be much more cost effective. The use of machine learning in addressing ambitious issues of widespread importance such as global warming and depleting underground water levels is promising with massive collection of relevant data.

"A breakthrough in machine learning would be worth ten Microsofts."
– Bill Gates

A number of different types of machine learning models exist today but the concept of machine learning largely boils down to three core components "representation", "evaluation" and "optimization". Here are some of the standard concepts that are applicable to all of them:

Representation

Machine learning models are incapable of directly hearing, seeing or sensing input examples. Therefore, a data representation is required to supply the model with a useful vantage point into the key qualities of the data. In order to successfully train a machine learning model selection of key features that best represent the data is very important.

"Representation" simply refers to the act of representing data points to the computing system in a language that it understands with the use of a set of classifiers. A classifier can be defined as "a system that inputs a vector of discrete and or continuous feature values and outputs a single discrete value called class". For a model to learn from the represented data the training data set or the "hypothesis space" must contain desired classifier that you want the models to be trained on. Any classifiers that are external to the hypothesis space cannot be learned by the model.

The data features used to represent the input are extremely crucial to the machine learning process. The data features are so critical to the development of desired machine learning model that it could easily be the key distinction between a successful and failed machine learning project. A training data set consisting of multiple independent features that are well correlated with the class can make the learning process much smoother. On the other hand, class consisting of complex features may not be easy to learn from for the machine. This usually needs the raw data to be processed to allow construction of desired features from it, which can be used for the machine learning model. The process of deriving features from raw data tends to be the most time consuming and laborious part of the ML project. It is also considered the highly creative and exciting part of the project where intuition and trial and error play just as important role as the technical requirements.

The process of ML is not a single-shot procedure of developing a training data set and executing it instead it's an iterative process that requires analysis of the post run results followed by modification of the training data set and then repeating the whole process all over again. Another contributing factor to the extensive time and effort required in engineering of the training data set is domain specificity. Training data set for an e-commerce platform to generate predictions based on consumer behavior analysis will be very different from the training data set required to develop a self-driving car. However, the actual machine learning process largely holds true across the industrial spectrum. No wonder, a lot of research is being done to automate the feature engineering process.

Evaluation

Essentially the process of judging multiple hypothesis or models to choose one model over another is referred to as an evaluation. To be able to differentiate between good quality classifiers from the lower quality classifiers, it is recommended to use an "evaluation function". This function is also known as "objective", "utility" or "scoring" function.

The machine learning algorithm has its own internal evaluation function which tends to be different from the external evaluation function used by the researchers to optimize the classifier. Normally the evaluation function will be defined prior to the selection of the data representation tool and tends to be the first step of the project. For example, the machine learning model for self-driving cars has a feature that allows identification of pedestrians in the car's vicinity at near zero false negatives and a low false positive, which are the evaluation functions and the pre-existing condition that needs to be "represented" using applicable data features.

Optimization

The process of searching the space of presented models to achieve better evaluations or highest scoring classifier is called as "optimization". For algorithms with multiple optimum classifiers, the selection of optimization technique is very important in determination of the classifier produced as well as to achieve a more efficient learning model. A variety of off-the-shelf optimizers are available in the market that will help you kick start a new machine learning model before eventually replacing them with a custom designed optimizers.

Basic Machine Learning Terminologies

Agent – In context of reinforcement learning, an agent refers to an entity that utilizes a policy to max out the expected return achieved with transition of different environment states.

Boosting – Boosting can be defined as a ML technique that would sequentially combine set of simple and low accuracy classifiers (known as "weak" classifiers) into a classifier which is highly accurate (known as "strong" classifier) by increasing the weight of the samples that are being classified wrongly by the model.

Candidate generation – The phase of selecting the initial set of suggestions provided by a recommendation system is referred to as candidate generation. For example, a book library can offer 540,000 titles. The "candidate generation phase" will produce a subset of few 100 books meeting the needs of a particular user and can be refined further to an even smaller set as needed.

Categorical Data – Data features boasting a distinct set of potential values is called as categorical data. For example, a categorical feature named TV model can have a discrete set of multiple possible values including Smart, Roku, Fire.

Checkpoint – Checkpoint can be defined as a data point that is capable of capturing the state of the variables at a specific moment in time of the ML model. With the use of checkpoints, training can be carried out across multiple sessions and model weights or scores can be exported.

Class – Class can be defined as "one of a set of listed target values for a given label". For instance, a learning model designed to detect email spams will have 2 classes, namely, "spam" and "not spam".

Classification model – The type of machine learning model used to differentiate between multiple distinct classes of the data is referred to as classification model. For example, a classification model for identification of dog breeds could assess whether the dog picture used as input is Labrador, Schnauzer, German Shepherd, Beagle and so on.

Collaborative filtering – The process of generating predictions for a particular user based on the shared interests of a group of similar users is called as collaborative filtering.

Continuous feature – It is defined as a "floating point feature with an infinite range of possible values".

Discrete feature – It is defined as a feature that can be given only a finite set of potential values and has no flexibility.

Discriminator – A system used to determine whether the input samples are realistic or not is called as discriminator.

Down-sampling – The process of Down-sampling refers to the process used to reduce the amount of info comprised in a feature or use of a remarkably low percent of classes that are overrepresented in an effort to train the ML model with higher efficiency.

Dynamic model – A learning model that is continuously receiving input data to be trained in a continuous manner is called as dynamic model.

Ensemble – A set of predictions created by combining predictions of more than one model is called as ensemble.

Environment – The term environment used in context of reinforcement machine learning constitutes "the world that contains the agent and allows the agent to observe that world's state".

Episode – The term episode used in context of reinforcement machine learning constitutes every sequential trial taken by the model to learn from its environment.

Feature – Any of the data variables that can be used as an input to generate predictions is called as a feature.

Feature engineering – Feature engineering can be defined as "the process of determining which features might be useful in training a model, and then converting raw data from log files and other sources into said features".

Feature extraction – Feature extraction can be defined as "the process of retrieving intermediate feature representations calculated by an unsupervised or pre-trained model for use in another model as input".

Few-shot learning - Few-shot learning can be defined as "a machine learning approach, often used for object classification, designed to learn effective classifiers from only a small number of training examples".

Fine tuning – The process of "performing a secondary optimization to adjust the parameters of an already trained model to fit a new problem" is called as fine tuning. It is widely used to refit the weights of a "trained unsupervised model" to a "supervised model".

Generalization – A machine learning model's capability to produce accurate predictions from fresh and unknown input data instead of the data set utilized during the training phase of the model is called as generalization..

Inference – In context of ML, the concept of inference pertains to the process of generating predictions with the application of the trained model to data sample that has not been labeled.

Label – In context of machine learning (supervised), the "answer" or "result" part of an example is called as label. All the examples in a dataset containing data that has already been labeled will comprise of single or multiple features accompanied by a label. For example, in a house dataset, these features could include the year built, no. of bedrooms and bathrooms, while the label can be the "house's price".

Linear model – Linear model is defined as a model that can assigns singular weight to each feature for generating predictions.

Loss – In context of ML, the concept of loss pertains to the measure of the extent by which the predictions produced by the model are not in line with its training labels.

Matplotlib – It is an open source Python 2-D plotting library that can be utilized to visualize various elements of machine learning.

Model – In context of machine learning, model refers to a representation of the learning and training that has been acquired by the system from the training dataset.

NumPy – Another open source data library that can provide efficient array operations in Python.

One-shot learning – In context of ML, one-shot learning can be defined as the machine learning approach that allows learning of effective classifiers from unique training sample and is frequently utilized classification of objects.

Overfitting - In context of machine learning, overfitting is referred to as production of a model that can match the training dataset extremely closely and renders the model inefficient in making accurate predictions on fresh input.

Parameter – Any variable of the ML model which would allow the machine learning system to self-learn independently is called as parameter.

Pipeline – In context of machine learning, pipeline refers to the infrastructure that surrounds a machine learning algorithm and comprises of a collection of data, any data additions made to the training data files, training of single or multiple models, and exporting the models into production.

Random forest – In context of machine learning, the concept of random forest pertains to an ensemble technique to find a decision tree that would most accurately fit the training dataset by creating two or more decision trees with a random selection of features.

Scaling - In context of machine learning, scaling refers to "a common feature engineering practice to tame a feature's range of values to match the range of other features in the dataset".

Sequence model - A sequence model simply refers to a model with sequential dependency on data inputs to generate a future prediction.

Underfitting – This refers to the process of generating a model with unacceptable predictive ability because the model has failed to capture the complexity of the training dataset.

Validation – The process of evaluating the quality of the ML model with the use of the validation set during the training phase of the model is called as validation. The main goal of this process is to make sure that the performance of the model can be applied beyond the training data.

Machine Learning Algorithms

Machine learning allows an analysis of large volumes of data and delivers faster and more accurate results. With proper training, this technology can allow organizations to identify profitable opportunities and business risks. Machine learning in combination with cognitive technologies and artificial intelligence tends to be even more effective and accurate in processing massive quantities of data. The machine learning algorithms can be categorized into four:

Supervised machine learning algorithms – These algorithms are capable of applying the lessons from the previous runs to new data set using labeled examples to successfully make predictions for future events. For example, a machine can be programmed with data points labeled as "F" (failed) or "S" (success). The learning algorithm will receive inputs with corresponding correct outputs and run a comparison of its own actual output against the expected or correct, in an attempt to identify errors that can be fixed to make the model more efficient and accurate. With sufficient training, the algorithms are capable of providing 'targets' for any new data input through methods like regression, classification, prediction, and ingredient boosting. The analysis starts from a known training data set and the machine learning algorithm then produces an "inferred function" to make future predictions pertaining to the output values. For example, the supervised learning algorithm-based systems are smart enough to anticipate and detect the likelihood of fraudulent credit card transactions being processed.

Unsupervised machine learning algorithms – These algorithms are used in the absence of classified and labeled training data sources. According to SAS, "Unsupervised Learning algorithms are used to study ways in which the system can infer a function to describe a hidden structure from unlabeled data i.e. to explore the data and identify some structure within". Similar to the supervised learning algorithms, these algorithms are able to explore the data and draw inferences from data sets, but cannot figure out the right output. For example, identification of individuals with similar shopping attributes, who can be segmented together and targeted with similar marketing campaigns. These algorithms are widely used to identify data outliers, provide product recommendations and segment text topics using techniques like "singular value decomposition", "self-organizing maps" and "k-means clustering".

Semi-supervised machine learning algorithms – As the name indicates, these algorithms fall somewhere in between supervised and unsupervised learning and are capable of using labeled as well as unlabeled data as training sources. A typical training set would include a majority of the unlabeled data with a limited volume of the labeled data. The systems running on semi-supervised learning algorithms with methods such as prediction, regression, and classification are able to significantly improve their learning accuracy. In situations where the acquired labeled data requires relevant and skilled resources for the machine to be able to train or learn from it, the semi-supervised learning algorithms are best suited. For example, identification of individual faces on a web camera.

Reinforcement Machine learning algorithms – These algorithms are capable of interacting with their environment by production of actions and discovery of errors or rewards. The primary characteristics of reinforcement learning are "trial and error research method and delayed reward". With the use of these algorithms, a machine can maximize its performance by automatically determining the ideal behavior within a specific context. Think of the reinforcement signal simply as a reward feedback that is required by the software agents or machines to help it learn which actions yield the fastest and accurate results. These algorithms are frequently used in robotics, gaming, and navigation.

Machine Learning in Practice

The complete process of machine learning is much more extensive than just the development and application of machine learning algorithms and can be divided into steps below:

1. Define the goals of the project taking into careful consideration all the prior knowledge and domain expertise available. Goals can easily become ambiguous since there are always additional things you want to achieve than practically possible to implement.

2. The data pre-processing and cleaning must result in a high-quality data set. This is the most critical and time-consuming step of the whole project. The larger the volume of data, the more noise it brings to the training data set which must be eradicated before feeding to the learner system.

3. Selection of appropriate learning model to meet the requirements of your project. This process tends to be rather simple given the variety types of data models available in the market.

4. Depending on the domain the machine learning model is applied to, the results may or may not require a clear understanding of the model by human experts as long as the model can successfully deliver desired results.

5. The final step is to consolidate and deploy the knowledge or information gathered from the model to be used on an industrial level.

6. The whole cycle from step 1 to 5 listed above is iteratively repeated until a result that can be used in practice is achieved.

Importance of Machine Learning

To get a sense of how significant machine learning is in our everyday lives, it is simpler to state what part of our cutting-edge way of life has not been touched by it. Each aspect of human life is being impacted by the "smart machines" intended to expand human capacities and improve efficiencies. Artificial Intelligence and machine learning technology is the focal precept of the "Fourth Industrial Revolution", that could possibly question our thoughts regarding being "human".

Here are few reasons to help you understand the significance of machine learning in our daily lives:

- Automation of repetitive learning and revelation from data. Not at all like hardware-driven robotic automation that simply automate manual assignments, machine learning allows performance of high volume, high volume, computer-based tasks consistently and dependably.

- Machine learning algorithms are helping Artificial Intelligence to adapt to the evolving world by allowing the machine or system to learn, take note and improve up on its prior errors. Machine learning algorithm functions as a classifier or a predictor to acquire new skills and identify data pattern and structure. For example, machine learning algorithm has generated a system that can teach itself how to play chess and even how to generate product recommendations based on customer activity and behavior data. The beauty of this model is that it adapts with every new set of data.

- Machine learning has made analysis of deeper and larger data set feasible with the use of neural networks containing multiple hidden layers. Think about it, a fraud detection system with numerous concealed layers would deem a work of fantasy just a couple of years ago. With the advent of big data and unlikely to envision computer powers, a whole new world is on the horizon. Data to the machines resembles the gas to the vehicle, the more data you can add to them, faster and more accurate results will get. Deep learning models flourish with abundance of data because they gain straightforwardly from the data.

- The "deep neural networks" of the machine learning algorithms have resulted in unbelievable accuracy. For example, frequent and repeated use of smart tech like "Amazon Alexa" and "Google Search", result in increased accuracy derived from deep learning. These "deep neural networks" are also empowering our medical field. Image classification and object recognition are now capable of finding cancer on MRIs with similar accuracy as that of a highly trained radiologist.

- Artificial Intelligence is allowing for enhanced and improved use of bid data analytics in conjunction with machine learning algorithms. Data has evolved as its own currency and when algorithms are self-learning it can easily become "intellectual property". The raw data is similar to a gold mine in that the more and deeper you dig, the more "gold" or valuable insight you can dig out or extract. Application of machine learning algorithms to the data can enable you to find the correct solutions quicker and makes for an upper hand. Keep in mind the best information will consistently win, despite the fact that everyone is utilizing comparative techniques.

Review Quiz

Answer the questions below to verify your understanding of the concepts explained in this chapter. The answer key can be found at the end of the quiz.

1. Name the 3 core concepts of the machine learning technology.

2. What is the process of selecting the initial set of recommendations called?

3. _____ is a set of predefined target values for an indicated label.

4. Name two open source machine learning libraries.

5. What function is used to distinguish between the good and bad classifiers?

6. The process of searching the space of presented models to achieve better evaluations or highest scoring classifier is called ____.

7. Name the system used to determined real input data from the fake input.

8. Come up with 3 labels for a dog dataset.

9. During the training phase of the ML model, the quality of the model may be checked by utilizing the process called ____.

10. The ____ revolution has resulted in development of Artificial Intelligence and machine learning technologies.

Answer Key

1. Representation, Evaluation and Optimization.
2. Candidate Generation.
3. Class.

4. NumPy, Matplotlib.

5. Evaluation Function.

6. Optimization.

7. Discriminator.

8. Breed, Color, Age. (any other data feature that will help you identify the dataset contains info on dogs can be used as a label)

9. Validation.

10. Fourth Industrial.

Chapter 2:

Introduction to Python

Python is a high-level programming language, commonly used for general purposes. It was originally developed by Guido van Rossum at the "Center Wiskunde & Informatica (CWI), Netherlands," in the 1980s and introduced by the "Python Software Foundation" in 1991. It was designed primarily to emphasize readability of programming code, and its syntax enables programmers to convey ideas using fewer lines of code. Python programming language increases the speed of operation while allowing for higher efficiency in creating system integrations. Developers are using Python for "web development (server-side), software development, mathematics, system scripting."

With the introduction of various enhancements such as "list comprehension" and a "garbage collection system," which can collect reference cycles, the Python 2.0 was launched in the last quarter of 2000. Subsequently, in 2008, Python 3.0 was released as a major version upgrade with backward compatibility allowing for the Python 2.0 code to be executed on Python 3.0 without requiring any modifications. Python is supported by a community of programmers that continually develop and maintain the "CPython," which is an open-source reference implementation. The "Python Software Foundation" is a not for profit organization that is responsible for managing and directing resources for developing Python programming as well as "CPython."

Here are some of the key features of Python that render it as the language of choice for coding beginners as well as advanced software programmers alike:

1. **Readability**: Python reads a lot like the English language, which contributes to its ease of readability.

2. **Learnability**: Python is a high-level programming language and considered easy to learn due to the ability to code using English language like expressions, which

implies it is simple to comprehend and thereby learn the language.

3. **Operating Systems**: Python is easily accessible and can be operated across different OS including Mac, Windows, Linux, Unix among others. This renders Python as a versatile and cross-platform language.

4. **Open Source**: Python is "open source", which means that the developer community can seamlessly make updates to the code, which are always available to anyone using Python for their software programming needs.

5. **Standardized Data Libraries**: Python features a big standard data library with a variety of useful codes and functionalities that can be used when writing Python code for data analysis and development of machine learning models. (Details on machine learning libraries will be provided later in this chapter)

6. **Free**: Considering the wide applicability and usage of Python, it is hard to believe that it continues to be freely available for easy download and use. This implies that anyone looking to learn or use Python can simply download and use it for their applications

completely free of charge. Python is indeed a perfect example of a "FLOSS (Free/Libre Open Source Software)", which means one could "freely distribute copies of this software, read its source code and modify it."

7. **Supports managing of exceptions**: An "exception" can be defined as "an event that can occur during program exception and can disrupt the normal flow of program." Python is capable of supporting handling of these "exceptions," implying that you could write fewer error-prone codes and test your code with a variety of cases, which could potentially lead to an "exception" in the future.

8. **Advanced Features**: Python can also support "generators and list comprehensions."

9. **Storage governance**: Python is also able to support "automatic memory management," which implies that the storage memory will be cleared and made available automatically. You are not required to clear and free up the system memory.

Installation Instructions for Python

You can follow the step by step instructions to download and install Python on a variety of operating systems. Simply jump to the section for the operating system you are working on. The latest version of Python released in the middle of the 2019 is Python 3.8.0. Make sure you are downloading and installing the most recent and stable version of Python and following the instructions below.

WINDOWS

1. From the official Python website, click on the "Downloads" icon and select Windows.

2. Click on the "Download Python 3.8.0" button to view all the downloadable files.

3. You will be taken to a different screen where you can select the Python version you would like to download. In this book, we will be using the Python 3 version under "Stable Releases." So scroll down the page and click on the "Download Windows x86-64 executable installer" link as shown in the picture below.

- Python 3.8.0 - Oct. 14, 2019

Note that Python 3.8.0 *cannot* be used on Windows XP or earlier.

- Download Windows help file
- Download Windows x86-64 embeddable zip file
- Download Windows x86-64 executable installer
- Download Windows x86-64 web-based installer
- Download Windows x86 embeddable zip file
- Download Windows x86 executable installer
- Download Windows x86 web-based installer

4. A pop-up window titled "python-3.8.0-amd64.exe" will be displayed.

5. Click on the "Save File" button to start downloading the file.

6. Once the download has completed, double click the saved file icon, and a "Python 3.8.0 (64-bit) Setup" pop window will be displayed.

7. Make sure that you select the "Install Launcher for all users (recommended)" and the "Add Python 3.8 to PATH" checkboxes. Note – If you already have an older version of Python installed on your system, the "Upgrade Now" button will appear instead of the "Install Now" button, and neither of the checkboxes will be displayed.

8. Click on the "Install Now" button and a "User Account Control" pop up window will be displayed.

9. A notification stating, "Do you want to allow this app to make changed to your device" will be displayed, click on Yes.

10. A new pop up window titled "Python 3.8.0 (64-bit) Setup" will be displayed containing a setup progress bar.

11. Once the installation has been completed, a "Set was successful" message will be displayed. Click on the Close button, and you are all set.

12. To verify the installation, navigate to the directory where you installed Python and double click on the python.exe file.

MACINTOSH

1. From the official Python website, click on the "Downloads" icon and select Mac.
2. Click on the "Download Python 3.8.0" button to view all the downloadable files.
3. You will be taken to a different screen where you can select the Python version you would like to download.

In this book, we will be using the Python 3 version under "Stable Releases." So scroll down the page and click on the "Download macOS 64-bit installer" link under Python 3.8.0, as shown in the picture below.

4. A pop-up window titled "python-3.8.0-macosx10.9.pkg" will be displayed.

5. Click on the "Save File" button to start downloading the file.

6. Once the download has completed, double click the saved file icon, and an "Install Python" pop window will be displayed.

7. Click on the "Continue" button to proceed, and a terms and conditions pop up window will be displayed.

8. Click Agree and then click on the "Install" button.

9. A notification requesting administrator permission and password will be displayed. Simply enter your system password to begin installation.

10. Once the installation has been completed, an "Installation was successful" message will be displayed. Click on the Close button, and you are all set.

11. To verify the installation, navigate to the directory where you installed Python and double click on the python launcher icon that will take you to the Python Terminal.

LINUX

- **For Red Hat, CentOS, or Fedora**, install the python3 and python3-devel packages.

- **For Debian or Ubuntu**, install the python3.x and python3.x-dev packages.

- **For Gentoo**, install the '=python-3.x*' ebuild (you may have to unmask it first).

1. From the official Python website, click on the "Downloads" icon and select Linux/UNIX.

2. Click on the "Download Python 3.8.0" button to view all the downloadable files.

3. You will be taken to a different screen where you can select the Python version you would like to download. In this book, we will be using the Python 3 version under "Stable Releases." So scroll down the page and click on the "Download Gzipped source tarball" link under Python 3.8.0, as shown in the picture below.

4. A pop-up window titled "python-3.7.5.tgz" will be displayed.

5. Click on the "Save File" button to start downloading the file.

6. Once the download has completed, double click the saved file icon, and an "Install Python" pop window will be displayed.

7. Follow the prompts on the screen to complete the installation process.

Getting Started

Now that you have the Python terminal installed on your computer, we will now see how you can start writing and executing the Python code. All Python codes are written in a text editor as (.py) files, which are then executed on the Python interpreter on the command line as shown in the code below, where "smallworld.py" is the name of the Python file:

"C: \Users\Your Name\python smallworld.py"
You can test a small code without writing the code in a file and simply executing it as a command-line itself by typing the code below on the Mac, Windows or Linux command line, as shown below:

"C: \Users\Your Name\python"

In case the above command doesn't work, you can use the code below instead

"C: \Users\Your Name\py"

Indentation – To understand the Python coding structure, you must first understand the significance of indentation or the number of spaces before you start typing the code. Unlike other coding languages where "indentation" is added to enhance the readability of the code, in Python, it is used to indicate a set of code. For example, look at the code below

If 7 > 4:

    print ('Seven is greater than 4')

There is indentation prior to the second line of code with the print command. If you skip the indentation and write the code as below, you will receive an error:

If 7 > 4:

print ('Seven is greater than 4')

The number of spaces can be adjusted but must be at least single-spaced. For example, you can execute the code below with higher indentation, but for a specific set of code same number of spaces must be used, or you will receive an error.

If 7 > 4:

      print ('Seven is greater than 4')

Adding Comments – In Python, you can add comments to the code by starting the code comment lines with a "#", as shown in the example below:

#Add any relevant comment here
print ('Planet Earth')

Comments are also used as a description of the code and not executed by the Python terminal. It is important to remember that if you put a comment at the end of code like the entire code line will be skipped by the Python terminal as shown in the code below. Comments are extremely useful in case you need to stop the execution when you are testing the code.

print ('Planet Earth')   #Add comments here

You can also add multiple lines of comments by starting each code line with "#," as shown below:

#Add comment here
#Supplement the comment here
#Further add the comment here
print ('Planet Earth')

Python Variables

In Python, variables are used to store data values without executing a command for it. You can create a variable by simply assigning desired value to it, as shown in the example below:

A = 110
B = 'David'
print (A)
print (B)

A variable may be declared without a specific data type. The data type of a variable can also be modified after its initial declaration, as shown in the example below:

A = 110 # A has data type set as int
A = 'David' # A now has data type str
print (A)

There are certain rules applied to the Python variable names as follows:

1. Variable names can be short as single alphabets or more descriptive words like height, weight, etc.

2. Variable names can only be started with an underscore character or a letter.

3. Variable names must not start with numbers.

4. Variable names may contain underscores or alphanumeric characters. No other special characters are allowed.

5. Variable names are case sensitive. For example, 'height,' 'Height' and 'HEIGHT' will be accounted as 3 separate variables.

Assigning Value to Variables

In Python, multiple variables can be assigned DISTINCT values in a single code line, as shown in the example below:

A, B, C = 'lilac,' 'red,' 'cyan'
print (A)
print (B)
print (C)

OR multiple variables can be assigned SAME value in a single code line, as shown in the example below:

A, B, C = 'lilac'
print (A)
print (B)
print (C)

Python Data Types

To further understand the concept of variables, let's first look at the Python data types. Python supports a variety of data types as listed below:

Category	Data Type	Example Syntax
Text	*"str"*	'Planet Earth' "Planet Earth" """Planet Earth"""
Boolean	*"bool"*	'True' 'False'
Mapping (mixed data types, associative array of key and value pairs)	*"dict"*	'{'key9' : 9.0, 6 : True}'
Sequence (may contain mixed data types)	*"list"*	'[9.0, 'character', True]'
	"tuple"	'[9.0, 'character', True]'
	"range"	'range (10, 50)' 'range (100, 50, 10, -10, -50, -100)'
Binary	*"bytes"*	b 'byte sequence' b 'byte sequence' bytes ([120, 90, 75, 100])
	"bytearray"	bytearray (b 'byte sequence') bytearray (b 'byte sequence') bytearray ([120, 90, 75, 100])
	"memoryview"	

Set (unordered, no duplicates, mixed data types)	*"set"*	'[9.0, 'character', True]'
	"frozenset"	'frozenset ([9.0, 'character', True])'
Numeric	*"int"*	'54'
	"float"	'18e9'
	"complex"	'18 + 3.1j'
Ellipsis (index in NumPy arrays)	*"ellipsis"*	'...' 'Ellipsis'

To view the data type of any object, you can use the *"type ()"* function as shown in the example below:

A = 'Lilac'

print (type (A))

Assigning the Data Type to Variables

As mentioned earlier, you can create a new variable by simply declaring a value for it. This set data value, in turn, assigns the data type to the variable.

To assign a specific data type to a variable, the constructor functions listed below can be used:

Constructor Functions	Data Type
A = *str ('Planet Earth)'*	str
A = *int (99)*	Int (Must be a whole number, positive or negative with no decimals, no length restrictions)
A = *float (15e6)*	Float (Floating point number must be a positive or negative number with one or more decimals; maybe scientific number an 'e' to specify an exponential power of 10)
A = *complex (99j)*	Complex (Must be written with a 'j' as an imaginary character)
A = *list (('cyan', 'red', 'olive'))*	list
A = *range (1, 100)*	range
A = *tuple (('cyan', 'red', 'olive'))*	tuple
A = *set (('cyan', 'red', 'olive'))*	set
A = *frozenset (('cyan', 'olive', 'red'))*	frozenset
A = *dict ('color' : 'red', 'year' : 1999)*	dict
A = *bool (False)*	bool
A = *bytes (54)*	bytes
A = *bytearray (8)*	bytearray
A = *memoryview (bytes (55))*	memoryview

EXERCISE – To solidify your understanding of data types. Look at the first column of the table below and write the data type for that variable. Once you have all your answers, look at the second column, and verify your answers.

Variable	Data Type
A = 'Planet Earth'	str
A = 99	int
A = 29e2	float
A = 99j	complex
A = ['cyan', 'red', 'olive']	list
A = range (1, 100)	range
A = ('cyan', 'red', 'olive')	tuple
A = {'cyan', 'red', 'olive'}	set
A = frozenset ({ 'cyan', 'olive', 'red'})	frozenset
A = ['color' : 'red', 'year' : 1999}	dict
A = False	bool
A = b 'Welcome'	bytes
A = bytearray (8)	bytearray
A = memoryview (bytes (55))	memoryview

Output Variables

In order to retrieve variables as output, the "print" statements are used in Python. You can use the "+" character to combine text with a variable for final output, as shown in the example below:

'A = 'red'

print ('Apples are' + A)'

OUTPUT – 'Apples are red'

A variable can also be combined with another variable using the "+" character as shown in the example below:

'A = 'Apples are'
B = 'red'
AB = A + B
print (AB)'

OUTPUT – 'Apples are red'

However, when the "+" character is used with numeric values, it retains its function as a mathematical operator, as shown in the example below:

'A = 20
B = 30
print (A + B)'

OUTPUT = 50

You will not be able to combine a string of characters with numbers and will trigger an error instead, as shown in the example below:

A = 'red'
B = 30
print (A + B)

OUTPUT – N/A – ERROR

Chapter 3:

Python Coding Basics

In the previous chapter, you learned the basics of Python syntax, the concept of Python Variables and Comments that serve as a prerequisite to the learning of Python programming. In this chapter, we will be looking at the nuances of how to write efficient and effective Python codes, focusing on various programming elements such as Booleans, Tuples, Sets, Dictionaries and much more. So let's get started.

Python Numbers

In Python programming, you will be working with 3 different numeric data types, namely, "int," "float" and "complex." In the previous chapter, you learned the details of what these data types entail, but below are some examples to refresh your memory.

Data Type	Example
Int (Must be a whole number, positive or negative with no decimals, no length restrictions)	*363 or 3.214*
Float (Floating point number must be a positive or negative number with one or more decimals; maybe scientific number an "e" to specify an exponential power of 10)	*29e3*
Complex (Must be written with a "j" as an imaginary character)	*92j*

EXERCISE – Create variable "a" with data value as "3.24", variable "b" with data value as "9e3" and variable "c" with data value as "-39j".

****USE YOUR DISCRETION HERE AND WRITE YOUR CODE FIRST****

Now, check your code against the correct code below:

```
a = 3.24        # int
b = 9e3         # float
c = -39j        # complex
```

```
print (type (a))
print (type (b))
```

print (type (c))

Note – The # comments are not required for the correct code and are only mentioned to bolster your understanding of the concept.

Converting One Numeric Data Type to Another

As all Python variables are dynamic in nature, you will be able to convert the data type of these variables if needed by deriving a new variable from the variable that you would like to assign a new data type.

Let's continue building on the exercise discussed above.

```
a = 3.24       # int
b = 9e3        # float
c = -39j       # complex
```

```
#conversion from int to float
x = float (a)
```

```
#conversion from float to complex
y = complex (b)
```

#conversion from complex to int

z = float (c)

#conversion from int to complex

x1 = int (a)

print (x)

print (y)

print (z)

print (x1)

print (type (x))

print (type (y))

print (type (z))

print (type (x1))

EXERCISE – View a random number between 14 and 24 by importing the random module.

****USE YOUR DISCRETION HERE AND WRITE YOUR CODE FIRST***

Now, check your code against the correct code below:

import random

print (random.randrange (14, 24))

Variable Casting with Constructor Functions

In the discussion and exercise above, you learned that variables could be declared by simply assigning desired data value to them and thereby the variables will assume the pertinent data type based on the data value. However, Python allows you to specify the data types for variables by using classes or "constructor functions" to define the data type for variables. This process is called "Casting."

Here are the 3 constructor functions used for "casting" numeric data type to a variable.

Constructor Functions	Data Type
int ()	Will construct an integer number from an integer literal, a string literal (provided the string is representing a whole number) or a float literal (by rounding down to the preceding whole number)
float ()	Will construct a float number from a string literal (provided the string is representing a float or an integer), a float literal or an integer literal
complex ()	Will construct a string from a large number of data types, such as integer literals, float literals, and strings

Here are some examples:

Integer:

a = int (6)   # a takes the value 6
b = int (4.6)   # b takes the value 4
c = int ('7')   # c takes the value 7

Float:

a = float (6)   # a takes the value 6.0
b = float (4.6)   # b takes the value 4.6
c = float ('7')   # c takes the value 7.0

String:

a = str ('serial')   # a takes the value 'serial'
b = str (4.6)   # b takes the value '4.6'
c = str ('7')   # c takes the value '7.0'

Python Strings

In Python, string data type for a variable is denoted by using single, double, or triple quotation marks. This implies that you can assign string data value to variable by quoting the string of characters. For example, "welcome" is the same as 'welcome' and '''welcome'''.

EXERCISE – Create a variable "v" with a string data value as "outfit is cyan" and display it.

****USE YOUR DISCRETION HERE AND WRITE YOUR CODE FIRST****

Now, check your code against the correct code below:

v = 'outfit is cyan'

print (v)

OUTPUT – outfit is cyan

EXERCISE – Create a variable "A" with a multiple-line string data value as "Looking at the sky tonight, thinking of you by my side! Let the world go on and on, it will be alright if I stay strong!" and display it.

****USE YOUR DISCRETION HERE AND WRITE YOUR CODE FIRST****

Now, check your code against the correct code below:

a = '''Loving another is never easy,
People tell you it won't be breezy!
You make your own decision,
Don't let the fear stop you from your persuasion!'''
print (a)

OUTPUT – Loving another is never easy,

People tell you it won't be breezy!
You make your own decision,
Don't let the fear stop you from your persuasion!'"

Note – You must use triple quote to create multiline string data values.

String Arrays

In Python, string data values are arrays of bytes that represent Unicode characters as true for most programming languages. But unlike other programming languages, Python lacks data type for individual characters, which are denoted as string data type with length of 1.

The first character of every string is given the position of 'o', and subsequently the subsequent characters will have the position as 1, 2, 3, and so on. In order to display desired characters from a string data value, you can use the position of the character enclosed in square brackets. For example, if you wanted to display the fifth character of the string data value "apple" of variable "x." You will use the command "print (x [4])"

EXERCISE – Create a variable "P" with a string data value as "brilliant" and display the fourth character of this string.

Now, check your code against the correct code below:

```
P = 'brilliant'
print (P [4])
```

OUTPUT – l

Slicing

If you would like to view a range of characters, you can do so by specifying the start and the end index of the desired positions and separating the indexes by a colon. For example, to view characters of a string from position 1 to position 3, your code will be *"print (variable [1:3])"*.

You can even view the characters starting from the end of the string by using "negative indexes" and start slicing the string from the end of the string. For example, to view characters of a string from position 4 to position 1, your code will be *"print (variable [-4 : -2])"*.

In order to view the length of the string, you can use the "len ()" function. For example, to view the length of a string, your code will be *"print (len (variable))."*

EXERCISE – Create a variable "P" with a string data value as "strive for success!" and display characters from position 3 to 6 of this string.

****USE YOUR DISCRETION HERE AND WRITE YOUR CODE FIRST****

Now, check your code against the correct code below:

P = 'strive for success!'
print (P [4 : 7])

OUTPUT – vef

EXERCISE – Create a variable "x" with a string data value as "coding is cool" and display characters from position 6 to 1, starting the count from the end of this string.

****USE YOUR DISCRETION HERE AND WRITE YOUR CODE FIRST****

Now, check your code against the correct code below:

x = 'coding is cool'
print (x [-6 : -2])
OUTPUT - isco

EXERCISE – Create a variable "z" with a string data value as "programming champ" and display the length of this string.

****USE YOUR DISCRETION HERE AND WRITE YOUR CODE FIRST****

Now, check your code against the correct code below:

z = 'programming champ'
print (len (z))

OUTPUT - 16

String Methods

There are various built-in methods in Python that can be applied to string data values. Here are the Python codes for some of the most frequently used string methods, using variable *"P = 'roses are red!'"*.

"strip ()" method – To remove any blank spaces at the start and the end of the string.

P = " roses are red! "
print (P.strip ())
OUTPUT – roses are red!

"lower ()" method – To result in all the characters of a string in lower case.

P = "ROSES are RED!"
print (P.lower ())

OUTPUT – roses are red!

"upper ()" method – To result in all the characters of a string in upper case.

P = "Roses are Red!"
print (P.upper ())

OUTPUT – ROSES ARE RED!
"replace ()" method – To replace select characters of a string.

P = "roses are red!"
print (P.replace ("roses", "apples"))

OUTPUT – apples are red!

"split ()" method – To split a string into substrings using comma as the separator.

P = "Roses, Apples"

print (P.split (","))

OUTPUT – ['Roses', 'Apples']

String Concatenation

There might be instances when you need to collate different string variables. This can be accomplished with the use of the "+" logical operator. Here's the syntax for this Python code:

X = "string1"

Y = "string2"

Z = X + Y

print (Z)

Similarly, below is the syntax to insert a blank space between two different string variables.

X = "string1"

Y = "string2"

Z = X + " " + Y

print (Z)

However, Python does not permit the concatenation of string variables with numeric variables. But can be accomplished with the use of the *"format ()"* method, which will format the executed arguments and place them in the string where the placeholders "{ }" are used. Here's the syntax for this Python code:

X = numeric
Y = "String"
print (Y. format (X))

EXERCISE – Create two variables "A" and "B" with string data values as "Let's have" and "some pizza!" and display them as a concatenated string.

****USE YOUR DISCRETION HERE AND WRITE YOUR CODE FIRST****

Now, check your code against the correct code below:

A = "Let's have"
B = "some pizza!"
C = A + B
print (C)

OUTPUT – Let's have some pizza!

EXERCISE – Create two variables "A" with string data values as "her lucky number is" and "B" with numeric data value as "18" and display them as a concatenated string.

****USE YOUR DISCRETION HERE AND WRITE YOUR CODE FIRST****

Now, check your code against the correct code below:

A = "her lucky number is"
B = "18"
print (A. format (B))

OUTPUT – her lucky number is 18

Python Booleans

In the process of developing a software program, there is often a need to confirm and verify whether an expression is true or false. This is where Python Boolean data type and data values are used. In Python, comparison and evaluation of two data values will result in one of the two Boolean values: "True" or "False."

Here are some examples of comparison statement of numeric data leading to Boolean value:

print (100 > 90)

OUTPUT – True

print (100 == 90)

OUTPUT – False

print (100 < 90)

OUTPUT – False

Let's look at the *"bool ()"* function now, which allows for evaluation of numeric data as well as string data resulting in "True" or "False" Boolean values.

print (bool (99))

OUTPUT - True

print (bool ("Welcome"))

OUTPUT - True

Here are some key points to remember for Booleans:

1. If a statement has some kind of content, it would be evaluated as "True."

2. All string data values will be resulting as "True" unless the string is empty.

3. All numeric values will be resulting as "True" except "0"

4. Lists, Tuples, Set and Dictionaries will be resulting as "True", unless they are empty.

5. Mostly empty values like (), [], {}, "", False, None and 0 will be resulting as "False".

6. Any object created with the "_len_" function that result in the data value as "0" or "False" will be evaluated as "False".

In Python there are various built-in functions function that can be evaluated as Boolean, for example, the "isinstance()" function which allows you to determine the data type of an object. Therefore, in order to check if an object is integer, the code will be as below:

X = 123

print (isinstance (X, int))

EXERCISE – Create two variables "X" with string data values as "Just do it!" and "Y" with numeric data value as "3.24" and evaluate them.

Now, check your code against the correct code below:

X = "Just do it!"
Y = 3.24

print (bool (X))
print (bool (Y)

OUTPUT –
True
True

Python Lists

In Python, lists are collections of data types that can be changed, organized and include duplicate values. Lists are written within square brackets, as shown in the syntax below.

X = ["string001", "string002", "string003"]
print (X)

The same concept of position applies to Lists as the string data type, which dictates that the first string is considered to be at position 0. Subsequently, the strings that will follow are given position 1, 2 and so on. You can selectively display desired string from a List by referencing the position of that string inside square bracket in the print command as shown below.

X = ["string001", "string002", "string003"]
print (X [2])

OUTPUT – [string003]

Similarly, the concept of **negative indexing** is also applied to Python List. Let's look at the example below:

X = ["string001", "string002", "string003"]
print (X [-2])

OUTPUT – [string002]

You will also be able to specify a **range of indexes** by indicating the start and end of a range. The result in values of such command on a Python List would be a new List containing only the indicated items. Here is an example for your reference.

X = ["string001", "string002", "string003", "string004",
"string005", "string006"]
print (X [2 : 4])

OUTPUT – ["string003", "string004"]

* Remember the first item is at position 0, and the final position of the range (4) is not included.

Now, if you do not indicate the start of this range, it will default to the position 0 as shown in the example below:

X = ["string001", "string002", "string003", "string004", "string005", "string006"]
print (X [: 3])

OUTPUT – ["string001", "string002", "string003"]
Similarly, if you do not indicate the end of this range it will display all the items of the List from the indicated start range to the end of the List, as shown in the example below:

X = ["string001", "string002", "string003", "string004", "string005", "string006"]
print (X [3 :])

OUTPUT – ["string004", "string005", "string006"]

You can also specify a **range of negative indexes** to Python Lists, as shown in the example below:

X = ["string001", "string002", "string003", "string004", "string005", "string006"]
print (X [-3 : -1])

OUTPUT – ["string004", "string005"]

* Remember the last item is at position -1, and the final position of this range (-1) is not included in the Output.

There might be instances when you need to **change the data value** for a Python List. This can be accomplished by referring to the index number of that item and declaring the new value. Let's look at the example below:

X = ["string001", "string002", "string003", "string004", "string005", "string006"]
X [3] = "newstring"
print (X)

OUTPUT – ["string001", "string002", "string003", "newstring," "string005", "string006"]

You can also determine the **length** of a Python List using the "len()" function, as shown in the example below:

X = ["string001", "string002", "string003", "string004",
"string005", "string006"]
print (len (X))

OUTPUT – 6

Python Lists can also be changed by **adding new items** to an existing list using the built-in "append ()" method, as shown in the example below:

X = ["string001", "string002", "string003", "string004"]
X.append ("newstring")
print (X)

OUTPUT – ["string001", "string002", "string003", "string004", "newstring"]

You can also, add a new item to an existing Python List at a specific position using the built-in "insert ()" method, as shown in the example below:

X = ["string001", "string002", "string003", "string004"]
X.insert (2, "newstring")
print (X)

OUTPUT – ["string001", "string002", "newstring", "string004"]

There might be instances when you need to **copy** an existing Python List. This can be accomplished by using the built-in "copy ( )" method or the "list ( )" method, as shown in the example below:

X = ["string001", "string002", "string003", "string004", "string005", "string006"]
Y = X.copy( )
print (Y)

OUTPUT – ["string001", "string002", "string003", "string004", "string005", "string006"]

X = ["string001", "string002", "string003", "string004", "string005", "string006"]
Y = list (X)
print (Y)

OUTPUT – ["string001", "string002", "string003", "string004", "string005", "string006"]

There are multiple built-in methods to **delete items** from a Python List.

- To selectively delete a specific item, the "remove ()" method can be used.

X = ["string001", "string002", "string003", "string004"]

X.remove ("string002")

print (X)

OUTPUT - ["string001", "string003", "string004"]

- To delete a specific item from the List, the "pop ()" method can be used with the position of the value. If no index has been indicated, the last item of the index will be removed.

X = ["string001", "string002", "string003", "string004"]

X.pop ( )

print (X)

OUTPUT - ["string001", "string002", "string003"]

- To delete a specific index from the List, the "del ()" method can be used, followed by the index within square brackets.

X = ["string001", "string002", "string003", "string004"]

del X [2]

print (X)

OUTPUT - ["string001", "string002", "string004"]

- To delete the entire List variable, the "del ()" method can be used, as shown below.

X = ["string001", "string002", "string003", "string004"]
del X

OUTPUT - .....

- To delete all the string values from the List without deleting the variable itself, the "clear ()" method can be used, as shown below.

X = ["string001", "string002", "string003", "string004"]
X.clear()
print (X)

OUTPUT – [ ]

Concatenation of Lists

You can join multiple lists with the use of the "+" logical operator or by adding all the items from one list to another using the "append ( )" method. The "extend ( )" method can be used to add a list at the end of another list. Let's look at the examples below to understand these commands.

X = ["string001", "string002", "string003", "string004"]
Y = [10, 20, 30, 40]

Z = X + Y

print (Z)

OUTPUT – ["string001", "string002", "string003", "string004", 10, 20, 30, 40]

X = ["string001", "string002", "string003", "string004"]
Y = [10, 20, 30, 40]

For x in Y:
X.append (x)

print (X)

OUTPUT – ["string001", "string002", "string003", "string004", 10, 20, 30, 40]
X = ["string001", "string002", "string003"]
Y = [10, 20, 30]

X.extend (Y)
print (X)

OUTPUT – ["string001", "string002", "string003", 10, 20, 30]

EXERCISE – Create a list "A" with string data values as "red, olive, cyan, lilac, mustard" and display the item at -2 position.

USE YOUR DISCRETION HERE AND WRITE YOUR CODE FIRST

Now, check your code against the correct code below:

A = ["red", "olive", "cyan", "lilac", "mustard"]
print (A [-2])

OUTPUT – ["lilac"]

EXERCISE – Create a list "A" with string data values as "red, olive, cyan, lilac, mustard" and display the items ranging from the string on the second position to the end of the string.

USE YOUR DISCRETION HERE AND WRITE YOUR CODE FIRST

Now, check your code against the correct code below:

A = ["red", "olive", "cyan", "lilac", "mustard"]
print (A [2 :])

OUTPUT – ["cyan", "lilac", "mustard"]

EXERCISE – Create a list "A" with string data values as "red, olive, cyan, lilac, mustard" and replace the string "olive" to "teal."

****USE YOUR DISCRETION HERE AND WRITE YOUR CODE FIRST****

Now, check your code against the correct code below:

A = ["red", "olive", "cyan", "lilac", "mustard"]
A [1] = ["teal"]

print (A)

OUTPUT – ["red", "teal", "cyan", "lilac", "mustard"]

EXERCISE – Create a list "A" with string data values as "red, olive, cyan, lilac, mustard" and copy the list "A" to create list "B."

****USE YOUR DISCRETION HERE AND WRITE YOUR CODE FIRST****

Now, check your code against the correct code below:

A = ["red", "olive", "cyan", "lilac", "mustard"]

B = A.copy ( )

print (B)

OUTPUT – ["red", "olive", "cyan", "lilac", "mustard"]

EXERCISE – Create a list "A" with string data values as "red, olive, cyan, lilac, mustard" and delete the strings "red" and "lilac."

****USE YOUR DISCRETION HERE AND WRITE YOUR CODE FIRST****

Now, check your code against the correct code below:

A = ["red", "olive", "cyan", "lilac", "mustard"]
del.A [0, 2]
print (A)

OUTPUT – ["olive", "cyan", "mustard"]

Python Tuples

In Python, Tuples are collections of data types that cannot be changed but can be arranged in specific order. Tuples allow for duplicate items and are written within round brackets, as shown in the syntax below.

Tuple = ("string001", "string002", "string003")
print (Tuple)

Similar to the Python List, you can selectively display the desired string from a Tuple by referencing the position of that string inside square bracket in the print command as shown below.

Tuple = ("string001", "string002", "string003")
print (Tuple [1])

OUTPUT – ("string002")

The concept of **negative indexing** can also be applied to Python Tuple, as shown in the example below:
Tuple = ("string001", "string002", "string003", "string004", "string005")
print (Tuple [-2])

OUTPUT – ("string004")

You will also be able to specify a **range of indexes** by indicating the start and end of a range. The result in values of such command on a Python Tuple would be a new Tuple containing only the indicated items, as shown in the example below:

*Tuple = ("string001", "string002", "string003", "string004",
"string005", "string006")*
print (Tuple [1:5])

OUTPUT – *("string002", "string003", "string004",
"string005")*

* Remember the first item is at position 0 and the final position of the range, which is the fifth position in this example, is not included.

You can also specify a **range of negative indexes** to Python Tuples, as shown in the example below:

*Tuple = ("string001", "string002", "string003", "string004",
"string005", "string006")*
print (Tuple [-4: -2])

OUTPUT – *("string004", "string005")*

* Remember the last item is at position -1 and the final position of this range, which is the negative fourth position in this example is not included in the Output.

Unlike Python lists, you cannot directly **change the data value of Python Tuples** after they have been created.

However, conversion of a Tuple into a List and then modifying the data value of that List will allow you to subsequently create a Tuple from that updated List. Let's look at the example below:

Tuple1 = ("string001", "string002", "string003",
"string004", "string005", "string006")
List1 = list (Tuple1)
List1 [2] = "update this list to create new tuple"
Tuple1 = tuple (List1)

print (Tuple1)

OUTPUT – ("string001", "string002", "update this list to create new tuple", "string004", "string005", "string006")

You can also determine the **length** of a Python Tuple using the "len()" function, as shown in the example below:

Tuple = ("string001", "string002", "string003", "string004",
"string005", "string006")
print (len (Tuple))

OUTPUT – 6

You cannot selectively delete items from a Tuple, but you can use the "del" keyword to **delete the Tuple** in its entirety, as shown in the example below:

Tuple = ("string001", "string002", "string003", "string004")
del Tuple

print (Tuple)

OUTPUT – name 'Tuple' is not defined

You can **join multiple Tuples** with the use of the "+" logical operator.

Tuple1 = ("string001", "string002", "string003", "string004")
Tuple2 = (100, 200, 300)

Tuple3 = Tuple1 + Tuple2
print (Tuple3)

OUTPUT – ("string001", "string002", "string003", "string004", 100, 200, 300)

You can also use the "tuple ( )" constructor to create a Tuple, as shown in the example below:

Tuple1 = tuple (("string001", "string002", "string003",
"string004"))
print (Tuple1)

EXERCISE – Create a Tuple "X" with string data values as "pies, cake, bread, scone, cookies" and display the item at -3 position.

****USE YOUR DISCRETION HERE AND WRITE YOUR CODE FIRST****

Now, check your code against the correct code below:

X = ("pies," "cake," "bread," "scone," "cookies")
print (X [-3])

OUTPUT – ("bread")

EXERCISE – Create a Tuple "X" with string data values as "pies, cake, bread, scone, cookies" and display items ranging from -2 to -4.

****USE YOUR DISCRETION HERE AND WRITE YOUR CODE FIRST****

Now, check your code against the correct code below:

X = ("pies," "cake," "bread," "scone," "cookies")
print (X [-4 : -2])

OUTPUT – ("cake," "bread")

EXERCISE – Create a Tuple "X" with string data values as "pies, cake, bread, scone, cookies" and change its item from "cookies" to "tart" using List function.

****USE YOUR DISCRETION HERE AND WRITE YOUR CODE FIRST****

Now, check your code against the correct code below:

X = ("pies", "cake", "bread", "scone", "cookies")
Y = list (X)
Y [4] = "tart"
X = tuple (Y)

print (X)

OUTPUT – ("pies," "cake," "bread," "scone," "tart")

EXERCISE – Create a Tuple "X" with string data values as "pies, cake, cookies" and another Tuple "Y" with numeric data values as (2, 12, 22), then join them together.

****USE YOUR DISCRETION HERE AND WRITE YOUR CODE FIRST****

Now, check your code against the correct code below:

X = ("pies," "cake," "cookies")
Y = (2, 12, 22)

Z = X + Y
print (Z)

OUTPUT – ("pies," "cake," "cookies," 2, 12, 22)

Python Sets

In Python, Sets are collections of data types that cannot be organized and indexed. Sets do not allow for duplicate items and must be written within curly brackets, as shown in the syntax below.

set = {"string1", "string2", "string3"}
print (set)

Unlike the Python List and Tuple, you cannot selectively display desired items from a Set by referencing the position of that item because the Python Set are not arranged in any order. Therefore, items do not have any indexing. However, the "for" loop can be used on Sets (more on this topic later in this chapter).

Unlike Python Lists, you cannot directly **change the data values of Python Sets** after they have been created. However, you can use the "add ()" method to add a single item to Set and use the "update ( )" method to one or more items to an already existing Set. Let's look at the example below:

set = {"string1", "string2", "string3"}
set. add ("newstring")
print (set)

OUTPUT – {"string1", "string2", "string3", "newstring"}

set = {"string1", "string2", "string3"}
set. update (["newstring1", "newstring2", "newstring3",)
print (set)

OUTPUT – {"string1", "string2", "string3", "newstring1", "newstring2", "newstring3"}

You can also determine the **length** of a Python Set using the "len()" function, as shown in the example below:

set = {"string1", "string2", "string3", "string4", "string5",
"string6", "string7"}
print (len(set))

OUTPUT – 7

To selectively **delete a specific item from a Set**, the "remove ()" method can be used as shown in the code below:

set = {"string1", "string2", "string3", "string4", "string5"}
set. remove ("string4")
print (set)

OUTPUT – {"string1", "string2", "string3", "string5"}

You can also use the "discard ( )" method to delete specific items from a Set, as shown in the example below:

set = {"string1", "string2", "string3", "string4", "string5"}
set. discard ("string3")
print (set)

OUTPUT – {"string1", "string2", "string4", "string5"}
The "pop ( )" method can be used to selectively delete only the last item of a Set. It must be noted here that since the Python Sets are unordered, any item that the system deems as the last

item will be removed. As a result, the output of this method will be the item that has been removed.

set = {"string1", "string2", "string3", "string4", "string5"}
A = set.pop ( )
print (A)
print (set)

OUTPUT –
String2
{"string1", "string3", "string4", "string5"}

To delete the entire Set, the "del" keyword can be used, as shown below.

set = {"string1", "string2", "string3", "string4", "string5"}
delete set
print (set)

OUTPUT – name 'set' is not defined

To delete all the items from the Set without deleting the variable itself, the "clear ()" method can be used, as shown below.

set = {"string1", "string2", "string3", "string4", "string5"} set.clear ( )

print (set)

OUTPUT – set ( )

You can **join multiple Sets** with the use of the "union ( )" method. The output of this method will be a new set that contains all items from both the sets. You can also use the "update ( )" method to insert all the items from one set into another without creating a new Set.

Set1 = {"string1", "string2", "string3", "string4", "string5"}
Set2 = {15, 25, 35, 45, 55}
Set3 = Set1.union (Set2)
print (Set3)

OUTPUT – {"string1", 15, "string2", 25, "string3", 35, "string4", 45, "string5", 55}

Set1 = {"string1", "string2", "string3", "string4", "string5"}
Set2 = {15, 25, 35, 45, 55}
Set1.update (Set2)
print (Set1)

OUTPUT – {25, "string1", 15, "string4",55, "string2", 35, "string3", 45, "string5"}

You can also use the "set ( )" constructor to create a Set, as shown in the example below:

Set1 = set (("string1", "string2", "string3", "string4",
"string5"))
print (Set1)

OUTPUT – {"string3", "string5", "string2", "string4", "string1"}

EXERCISE – Create a Set "Veg" with string data values as "pies, cake, bread, scone, cookies" and add new items "tart," "custard" and "waffles" to this Set.

****USE YOUR DISCRETION HERE AND WRITE YOUR CODE FIRST****

Now, check your code against the correct code below:

Veg = {"pies," "cake," "bread," "scone," "cookies"}
Veg.update (["tart," "custard," "waffles"])
print (Veg)

OUTPUT – {"pies," "custard," "scone," "cake," "bread," "waffles," "cookies," "tart"}

EXERCISE – Create a Set "Veg" with string data values as "pies, cake, bread, scone, cookies," then delete the last item from this Set.

Now, check your code against the correct code below:

Veg = {"pies", "cake", "bread", "scone", "cookies"}
X = Veg.pop ( )
print (X)
print (Veg)

OUTPUT –
bread
{"pies," "scone," "cake," "cookies"}

EXERCISE – Create a Set "Veg" with string data values as "pies, cake, bread, scone, cookies" and another Set "Veg2" with items as "tart, eggos, custard, waffles." Then combine both these Sets to create a third new Set.

****USE YOUR DISCRETION HERE AND WRITE YOUR CODE FIRST****

Now, check your code against the correct code below:

Veg = {"pies," "cake," "bread," "scone," "cookies"}
Veg2 = {"tart", "eggos", "custard", "waffles"}

AllVeg = Veg.union (Veg2)   #this Set name may vary
as it has not been defined in the exercise

print (AllVeg)

OUTPUT – {"pies", "custard", "scone", "cake", "eggos", "bread", "waffles", "cookies", "tart"}

Python Dictionary

In Python, Dictionaries are collections of data types that can be changed and indexed but are not arranged in any order. Each item in a Python Dictionary will comprise a key and its value. Dictionaries do not allow for duplicate items and must be written within curly brackets, as shown in the syntax below.

dict = {
"key01": "value01",
"key02": "value02",
"key03": "value03",
}
print (dict)

You can selectively display desired item value from a Dictionary by referencing its key inside square brackets in the print command as shown below.

dict = {
"key01": "value01",
"key02": "value02",
"key03": "value03",
}

X = dict ["key02"]
print (X)

OUTPUT – value02

You can also use the "get ( )" method to view the value of a key, as shown in the example below:

dict = {
"key01": "value01",
"key02": "value02",
"key03": "value03",
}

X = dict.get ("key01")

print (X)

OUTPUT – value01

There might be instances when you need to **change the value** of a key in a Python Dictionary. This can be accomplished by referring to the key of that item and declaring the new value. Let's look at the example below:

dict = {
"key01": "value01",
"key02": "value02",
"key03": "value03",
}

dict ["key03"] = "NEWvalue"
print (dict)

OUTPUT – {"key01": "value01", "key02": "value02", "key03": "NEWvalue"}

You can also determine the **length** of a Python Dictionary using the "len()" function, as shown in the example below:

dict = {
"key01": "value01",

"key02": "value02",
"key03": "value03",
"key04": "value04",
"key05": "value05"
}

print (len (dict))

OUTPUT – 5

Python Dictionary can also be changed by **adding** new index key and assigning a new value to that key, as shown in the example below:

dict = {
"key01": "value01",
"key02": "value02",
"key03": "value03",
}

dict ["NEWkey"] = "NEWvalue"
print (dict)

OUTPUT – {"key01": "value01", "key02": "value02",
"key03": "value03", "NEWkey": "NEWvalue"}

There are multiple built-in methods to **delete items** from a Python Dictionary.

- To selectively delete a specific item value, the "pop ()" method can be used with the indicated key name.

dict = {
"key01": "value01",
"key02": "value02",
"key03": "value03",
}
dict.pop ("key01")
print (dict)

OUTPUT – { "key02": "value02", "key03": "value03"}

- To selectively delete the item value that was last inserted, the "popitem ()" method can be used with the indicated key name.

dict = {
"key01": "value01",
"key02": "value02",
"key03": "value03",
}
dict.popitem ( )

print (dict)

OUTPUT – { "key01": "value01", "key02": "value02"}

- To selectively delete a specific item value, the "del" keyword can also be used with the indicated key name.

dict = {
"key01": "value01",
"key02": "value02",
"key03": "value03",
}
del dict ("key03")
print (dict)

OUTPUT – { "key01": "value01", "key02": "value02"}

- To delete a Python Dictionary in its entirety, the "del" keyword can also be used as shown in the example below:

dict = {
"key01": "value01",
"key02": "value02",
"key03": "value03",
}

del dict

print (dict)

OUTPUT – name 'dict' is not defined

- To delete all the items from the Dictionary without deleting the Dictionary itself, the "clear ()" method can be used as shown below.

dict = {

"key01": "value01",

"key02": "value02",

"key03": "value03",

}

dict.clear ( )

print (dict)

OUTPUT – { }

There might be instances when you need to **copy** an existing Python Dictionary. This can be accomplished by using the built-in "copy ( )" method or the "dict ( )" method, as shown in the examples below:

dict = {

"key01": "value01",

```
"key02": "value02",
"key03": "value03",
}
newdict = dict.copy ( )
print (newdict)
```

```
OUTPUT – {"key01": "value01", "key02": "value02",
"key03": "value03"}
```

```
Olddict = {
"key01": "value01",
"key02": "value02",
"key03": "value03",
}
newdict = dict (Olddict )
print (newdict)
```

```
OUTPUT – {"key01": "value01", "key02": "value02",
"key03": "value03"}
```

There is a unique feature that supports multiple Python Dictionaries to be **nested** within another Python Dictionary. You can either create a Dictionary containing child Dictionaries, as shown in the example below:

```
WendysFamilyDict = {
```

"burger1" : {
"name" : "Hamburger",
"price" : 2.99
},
"burger2" : {
"name" : "Cheeseburger",
"price" : 5
},
"burger3" : {
"name" : "Bigburger",
"price" : 1.99
}
}
print (WendysFamilyDict)

OUTPUT - {"burger1" : { "name" : "Hamburger", "price" : 2.99}, "burger2" : {"name" : "Cheeseburger", "price" : 5}, "burger3" : {"name" : "Bigburger", "price" : 1.99}}

Or you can create a brand-new Dictionary that contain other Dictionaries already existing on the system; your code will look like the one below:

burgerDict1 : {
"name" : "Hamburger,"
"price" : 2.99

```
}

burgerDict2 : {
“name” : “Cheeseburger”,
“price” : 5
}


burgerDict3 : {
“name” : “Bigburger”,
“price” : 1.99
}


WendysFamilyDict = {
“burgerDict1” : burgerDict1,
“burgerDict2” : burgerDict2
“burgerDict3” : burgerDict3
}
print (WendysFamilyDict)


OUTPUT - {“burger1” : { “name” : “Hamburger”, “price” : 2.99}, “burger2” : {“name” : “Cheeseburger”, “price” : 5}, “burger3” : {“name” : “Bigburger”, “price” : 1.99}}
```

Lastly, you can use the “dict ( )” function to create a new Python Dictionary. The key differences when you create items for the Dictionary using this function are 1. Round brackets are used instead of the curly brackets. 2. Equal to sign is used instead of the semi-colon. Let's look at the example below:

DictwithFunction = dict (key01 = "value01", key02 = "value02", key03 = "value03")
print (DictwithFunction)

OUTPUT – {"key01": "value01", "key02": "value02", "key03": "value03"}

EXERCISE – Create a Dictionary "Hortons" with items containing keys as "type," "size" and "price" with corresponding values as "cappuccino," "grande" and "4.99". Then add a new item with key as "syrup" and value as "hazelnut."

****USE YOUR DISCRETION HERE AND WRITE YOUR CODE FIRST****

Now, check your code against the correct code below:

```
Hortons = {
"type" : "cappuccino",
"size" : "grande",
"price" : 4.99
}
```

Hortons ["syrup"] = "hazelnut"

print (Hortons)

OUTPUT – {"type" : "cappuccino", "size" : "grande", "price" : 4.99, "syrup" : "hazelnut"}

EXERCISE – Create a Dictionary "Hortons" with items containing keys as "type," "size," and "price" with corresponding values as "cappuccino," "grande" and "4.99". Then use a function to remove the last added item.

****USE YOUR DISCRETION HERE AND WRITE YOUR CODE FIRST****

Now, check your code against the correct code below:

```
Hortons = {
"type" : "cappuccino",
"size" : "grande",
"price" : 4.99
}
Hortons.popitem ( )
print (Hortons)
```

OUTPUT – {"type" : "cappuccino", "size" : "grande"}

EXERCISE – Create a Dictionary "Hortons" with nested dictionary as listed below:

Dictionary Name	Key	Value
Coffee01	name	cappuccino
	size	venti
Coffee02	name	frappe
	size	grande
Coffee03	name	macchiato
	size	small

****USE YOUR DISCRETION HERE AND WRITE YOUR CODE FIRST****

Now, check your code against the correct code below:

```
Hortons = {
"coffee01" : {
"name" : "cappuccino",
"size" : "venti"
},
"coffee02" : {
"name" : "frappe",
"size" : "grande"
},
"coffee03" : {
```

"name" : "macchiato",

"size" : "small"

}

}

print (Hortons)

OUTPUT - {"coffee01" : { "name" : "cappuccino", "size" : "venti"}, "coffee02" : {"name" : "frappe", "size" : "grande"}, "coffee03" : {"name" : "macchiato", "size" : "small"}}

EXERCISE – Use the "dict ()" function to create a Dictionary "Hortons" with items containing keys as "type," "size" and "price" with corresponding values as "cappuccino," "grande" and "4.99".

USE YOUR DISCRETION HERE AND WRITE YOUR CODE FIRST

Now, check your code against the correct code below:

Hortons = dict (type = "cappuccino", size = "grande", price = 4.99}

print (Hortons)

OUTPUT – {"type" : "cappuccino", "size" : "grande", "price" : 4.99, "syrup" : "hazelnut"}

Chapter 4:

Advance Python Concepts

Python Conditions and If Statement

Python allows the usage of multiple mathematical, logical conditions as listed below:

- Equal to – "a == y"
- Not equal – "a !=y"
- Less than – "a < y"
- Less than, equal to – "a <= y"
- Greater than – "a > y"
- Greater than, equal to – "a >=y"

If Statement

All these conditions can be used within loops and **"if statement"**. The "if" keyword must be used to write these statements, as shown in the syntax below:

```
X = numeric1
Y = numeric2
if X > Y:
        print ("X is greater than Y")
```

The most important thing to remember here is that the indentation or the blank space at the beginning of a line in the code above is critical. Unlike other programming languages that use curly brackets, Python programming is driven by indentation in the process of defining the scope of the code. Therefore, writing the Python code below will result in an error.

```
X = numeric1
Y = numeric2
if X > Y:
print ("X is greater than Y")          #leads to an error
```

Else-If Statement

You can use the "elif" keyword to evaluate if the preceding condition is not true, then execute the subsequent condition. Here is the syntax followed by an example to help you understand this concept further:

```
X = numeric1
Y = numeric2
```

```
if X > Y:
        print ("X is greater than Y")
elif X == Y:
        print ("X and Y are equal")
```

Example:

```
X = 58
Y = 58
if X > Y:
        print ("X is greater than Y")
elif X == Y:
        print ("X and Y are equal")
```

OUTPUT - X and Y are equal

Else Statement

You can use the "else" keyword to execute any condition if the preceding conditions are not true. Here is the syntax followed by an example to help you understand this concept further:

```
X = numeric1
Y = numeric2
if X > Y:
        print ("X is greater than Y")
elif X == Y:
```

        print ("X and Y are equal")
else:
        print ("Y is greater than X")

Example:

X = 58
Y = 59
if X > Y:
        print ("X is greater than Y")
elif X == Y:
        print ("X and Y are equal")
else:
        print ("Y is greater than X")

OUTPUT - Y is greater than X

Alternatively, you can use the "else" keyword without using the "elif" keyword, as shown in the example below:

X = 69
Y = 96
if X > Y:
        print ("X is greater than Y")
else:
        print ("X is not greater than Y")

OUTPUT - X is not greater than Y

Single Line If Statement

You could even execute single line statements with "If" clause, as shown in the syntax below:

If x > y: print ("y is greater than x")

Single Line If-Else Statement

You could even execute single line statements with "If - Else" clause, as shown in the syntax below:

x = 10

y = 15

print ("x") If x > y else print ("y")

Single Line If-Else Statement with Multiple Else

You will also be able to execute single line statements with "If - Else" clause containing multiple "Else" statements in the same line, as shown in the syntax below:

x = 100

y = 100

print ("x") If x > y else print ("=") if a == b else print ("y")

"And" Keyword

If you are looking to combine multiple conditional statements, you can do so with the use of the "and" keyword, as shown in the example below:

x = 20

y = 18

z = 35

if x > y and z > x :

      print ("All conditions are True")

"Or" Keyword

If you are looking to combine multiple conditional statements, the other way you can do so is with the use of the "or" keyword, as shown in the example below:

x = 20

y = 18

z = 35

if x > y or x > z :

      print ("At least one of the conditions is True")

"Nested If" Statements

You can have multiple "if" statements within an "if" statement, as shown in the example below:

x = 110

if x > 50:

    print ("Greater than 50, ")

if x > 90:

    print ("and greater than 100")

else:

    print ("Not greater than 100")

"Pass" Statements

In Python, if you ever need to execute "if" statements without any content, you must incorporate a "pass" statement to avoid triggering any error. Here is an example to further your understanding of this concept.

x = 20

y = 55

if y > x

  pass

EXERCISE – Write the code to check if X = 69 is greater than Y = 79, the output should read "X is greater than Y." If the first condition is not true, then check if X is equal to Y, the output should read "X and Y are equal" otherwise the output should read "Y is greater than X."

****USE YOUR DISCRETION HERE AND WRITE YOUR CODE FIRST****

Now, check your code against the correct code below:

X = 69

Y = 79

if X > Y:

    print ("X is greater than Y")

elif X == Y:

    print ("X and Y are equal")

else:

    print ("Y is greater than X")

OUTPUT – "Y is greater than X"

EXERCISE – Write the code to check if x = 69 is greater '50', the output should read "Greater than 50". Then check if x is greater than '60', the output should read "And greater than 60", otherwise the output should read "Not greater than 60".

****USE YOUR DISCRETION HERE AND WRITE YOUR CODE FIRST****

Now, check your code against the correct code below:

x = 69

if x > 50:

    print ("Greater than 50")

if x > 60:

    print ("And greater than 60")

else:

    print ("Not greater than 60")

OUTPUT –

"Greater than 50"

"And greater than 60"

EXERCISE – Write the code to check if x = 9 is greater than y = 19 as well as if z = 25 is greater than x. The output should read if one or both the conditions are true.

****USE YOUR DISCRETION HERE AND WRITE YOUR CODE FIRST****

Now, check your code against the correct code below:

x = 9

y = 19

z = 25

if x > y and z > x :

   print ("Both the conditions are True")

OUTPUT – "Both the conditions are True"

EXERCISE – Write the code to check if x = 45 is less than y = 459 or z = 1459 is less than x. The output should read if one or both the conditions are true.

****USE YOUR DISCRETION HERE AND WRITE YOUR CODE FIRST****

Now, check your code against the correct code below:

x = 45

y = 459

z = 1459

if x < y and z < x :

   print ("At least one of the conditions is True")

OUTPUT – "At least one of the conditions is True"

Python "While" Loop

Python allows the usage of one of its standard loop commands i.e. "while" loop for execution of a block of statements, given that the initial condition holds true.

Here is the syntax for "while" loop statements:

p = num1
while p < num2:
    print (p)
    p += 1

In the syntax above, to prevent the loop from continuing with no end, the variable (p) was limited by setting to an increment. It is a pre-requisite for the "while" loop to index the variable in the statement.

"Break" Statements

These statements allow exiting from the "while" loop, even if the set condition holds true. In the example below, the variable will exit the loop when it reaches 4:

p = 2
while p < 7:
    print (p)
    if p == 4
      break
    p += 2

OUTPUT –

2

3

4

"Continue" Statements

These statements allow the system to stop the execution of the current condition and move to the next iteration of the loop. In the example below, system will continue the execution of the subsequent command if the variable equals 2:

```
p = 1
while p < 5:
        p += 1
        if p == 2:
            continue
        print (p)
```

OUTPUT –

1

3

4

5

(Note - The number 2 is missing from the result above)

"Else" Statement

The "else" statement allows you to execute a set of code after the "while" condition doesn't hold true any longer. The output in the example below will include a statement that the initial condition is no longer true:

p = 1
while p < 5:
>*print (p)*
>
>*p += 1*

else:
>*print ("p is no longer less than 5")*

OUTPUT –

1

2

3

4

p is no longer less than 5

EXERCISE – Write the code to print a series of number if x = 1 is smaller than 7.

****USE YOUR DISCRETION HERE AND WRITE YOUR CODE FIRST****

Now, check your code against the correct code below:

```
x = 1
while x < 7:
        print (x)
        x += 1
```

OUTPUT –

1

2

3

4

5

6

EXERCISE – Write the code to print a series of number if x = 1 is smaller than 6 and exit the loop when x is 3.

****USE YOUR DISCRETION HERE AND WRITE YOUR CODE FIRST****

Now, check your code against the correct code below:

```
x = 1
while x < 6:
        print (x)
```

```
    if x == 3
        break
    x += 1
```

OUTPUT –

1

2

3

EXERCISE – Write the code to print a series of number if x = 1 is smaller than 6 and continue to execute the initial condition if x is 3 in a new iteration.

Now, check your code against the correct code below:

```
x = 1
while x < 6:
    x += 1
    if x == 3:
    continue
    print (x)
```

OUTPUT –

1

2

4

5

6

(Note – The number 3 is missing, but the initial condition is executed in a new iteration.)

EXERCISE – Write the code to print a series of number if x = 1 is smaller than 4. Once this condition turns false, print "x is no longer less than 4".

USE YOUR DISCRETION HERE AND WRITE YOUR CODE FIRST

Now, check your code against the correct code below:

```
x = 1
while x < 4:
        print (x)
        x = 1
else:
        print ("x is no longer less than 4")
```

OUTPUT –

1

2

3

x is no longer less than 4

Python "For" Loop

Another one of the Python standard loops is "for" loop, which is used to execute iterations over a series such as string, tuple, set, dictionary, list. The "for" keyword in Python functions like an iterator found in object-oriented programming languages. It allows the execution of a block of statements once for every single item of tuple, set, list, and other series.

Let's look at the example below:

veg = ["tart," "scone," "cookies"]
for X in veg:
        print (X)

OUTPUT –
tart

scone

cookies

You will notice that in the code above that the variable was not defined. The "for" loop can be executed without setting an index for the variable in the code.

Loops for String

Python strings constitute a series of characters are iterative in nature. So if you wanted to loop through characters of a string, you could simply use the "for" loop as shown in the example below:

for X in "carrot":
        print (X)

OUTPUT –
c
a
r
r
o
t

"Break" Statements

If you want to exit the loop prior to its completion, you can use the "break" statements as shown in the example below:

veg = ["tart," "scone," "cookies," "pies," "carrot"]

for X in veg:

> *print (X)*
> *if X == "pies":*
> *break*

OUTPUT –

tart

scone

cookies

pies

In the example below, the print command was executed prior to the "break" statement and directly affected the output:

veg = ["tart," "scone," "cookies," "pies," "carrot"]
for X in veg:

> *if X == "pies":*
>> *break*

print (X)

OUTPUT –

tart

scone

cookies

"Continue" Statements

Similar to the "while" loop, the "continue" statements in the "for" loop is used to stop the execution of the current condition and move to the next iteration of the loop. Let's looks at the example below to further understand this concept:

veg = ["tart," "scone," "cookies," "pies," "carrot"]
for X in veg:
      if X == "cookies":
            continue
print (X)

OUTPUT –
tart
scone
pies
carrot

"Range" Function

The "range ( )" function can be used to loop through a block of code for a specific number of times. This function will result in a series of number beginning with "0" by default, with regular increments of 1 and ending at a specific number.

Here is an example of this function:

for X in range (5):

     print (X)

OUTPUT –

0

1

2

3

4

Note – The "range ( )" function defaulted to 0 as the first output, and the final value of the range, 5, is excluded from the output.

Let's look at another example with a start and end value of the "range ( )" function:

for X in range (1, 5):

     print (X)

OUTPUT –

1

2

3

4

In the example below, we will specify the increment value, which is set to 1 by default:

for X in range (3, 20, 5):

   print (X)

OUTPUT –

3

8

13

18

"Else" in "For" Loop

You can use the "else" keyword to specify a set of code that need to be executed upon the completion of the loop, as shown in the example below:

for X in range (5):

   print (X)

else:

   print ("The loop was completed")

OUTPUT –

0

1

2

3

4

The loop was completed

"Nested" Loops

When loops are defined within a loop, execution of the inner loop will occur once for each iteration of the outer loop. Let's look at the example below, where we want every single adjective must be printed for each listed vegetable:

adjective = ["olive," "leafy," "healthy"]

veg = ["spinach," "kale," "asparagus"]

for X in adjective:

    for Y in veg:

        print (X, Y)

OUTPUT –

olive spinach

olive kale

olive asparagus

leafy spinach

leafy kale

leafy asparagus

healthy spinach

healthy kale

healthy asparagus

"Pass" Statements

In Python, if you ever need to execute "for" loops without any content, you must incorporate a "pass" statement to avoid triggering any error. Here is an example to further your understanding of this concept.

for X in [1, 2, 3]
   pass

OUTPUT - ......
The empty "for" loop code above would have resulted in an error without the "pass" statement.

EXERCISE – Write the code to loop through a list of colors ("cyan," "lilac," "red") without defining a variable. Then loop through the characters of the string "cyan."

USE YOUR DISCRETION HERE AND WRITE YOUR CODE FIRST

Now, check your code against the correct code below:

colors = ["cyan," "lilac," "red"]
for A in colors:

print (A)
for B in "cyan":
        print (B)

OUTPUT –

cyan

lilac

red

c

y

a

n

EXERCISE – Write the code to loop through a list of colors ("cyan," "lilac," "red," "white") without defining a variable. Then break the loop at "red," without printing it in the result.

****USE YOUR DISCRETION HERE AND WRITE YOUR CODE FIRST****

Now, check your code against the correct code below:

colors = ["cyan", "lilac", "red", "white"]
for A in colors:
        if A == "red":

        break

      print (A)

OUTPUT –

cyan

lilac

EXERCISE – Write the code to loop through a range of numbers starting with 5 and ending with 30. Make sure to define the increments at 6.

****USE YOUR DISCRETION HERE AND WRITE YOUR CODE FIRST****

Now, check your code against the correct code below:

```
for X in range (5, 30, 6):
        print (X)
```

OUTPUT –

5

11

16

22

28

EXERCISE – Write the code to loop phones ("iPhone," "Samsung," "Google"), and loop that with colors ("black," "white," "gold") using nested loops.

****USE YOUR DISCRETION HERE AND WRITE YOUR CODE FIRST****

Now, check your code against the correct code below:

colors = ["black," "white," "gold"]
phones = ["iPhone," "Samsung," "Google"]

for X in colors:
    for Y in phones:
    print (X, Y)

OUTPUT –
black iPhone
black Samsung
black Google
white iPhone
white Samsung
white Google
gold iPhone
gold Samsung

gold Google

Python Classes and Objects

Python is one of the many object-oriented coding languages. Every entity of Python can be considered an object and has its own methods and properties. In Python, Classes are used to construct these objects serving as object blueprints.

A Python Class can be created using the keyword "class" with a predefined property (p) as shown in the syntax below:

class ClassName:

    p = 2

A Python Object can then be created from the Python Class created above, as shown in the syntax below:

Object1 = ClassName ( )
print (object1.p)

Built-in Function

In reality, creation of classes and objects is much more complex than the basic syntax provided above. This is where a built-in function to create classes called "__init__()" is used. When the classes are being created, this inherent class function is executed with it. The "__init__()" function is mostly used for assigning values to object properties and other actions that are required for creation of an object. Let's look at the example below to understand this function:

class Vehicle:

 def __init__ (self, name, year)

 self.name = name

 self.name = year

v1 = Vehicle ("AUDI", 2018)

print (v1.name)

print (v1.year)

OUTPUT – AUDI 2018

Object Methods

There are certain methods that can be created with the Python Objects. These methods can be considered as functions of that object. For example, to create a function that would print a comment regarding ownership of the vehicle and executed on the object v1, the command below will be used:

class Vehicle:

 def __init__ (self, name, year)

 self.name = name

 self.name = year

def newfunc (ownership):

print ("I am a proud owner of " + self.name)

v1 = Vehicle ("AUDI", 2018)

v1.newfunc ()

OUTPUT – I am a proud owner of AUDI

Reference Parameter

To refer to the latest instance of a class, the "self" parameter is used. It allows you to access variables that have been derived from a class. This parameter can be named as needed and does not have to be named "self". The important thing to remember here is that the first parameter defined for a class will become the reference parameter for that class, as shown in the example below:

class Vehicle:

def __init__ (refobject, name, year)

refobject.name = name

refobject.name = year

def newfunc (xyz):

print ("I am a proud owner of " + xyz.name)

v1 = Vehicle ("AUDI", 2018)

v1.newfunc ()

OUTPUT – I am a proud owner of AUDI

There might be instances when you need to **change the properties** of an object. You can easily do so by declaring the new property of the object as shown in the example below:

class Vehicle:

> *def __init__ (refobject, name, year)*
> *refobject.name = name*
> *refobject.name = year*

def newfunc (xyz):

> *print ("I am a proud owner of " + xyz.name)*

v1 = Vehicle ("AUDI", 2018)
v1.year = 2019

You can use the "del" keyword to selectively **remove properties of an object**, as shown in the example below:

class Vehicle:

> *def __init__ (refobject, name, year)*
> *refobject.name = name*
> *refobject.name = year*

def newfunc (xyz):

    print ("I am a proud owner of " + xyz.name)

v1 = Vehicle ("AUDI", 2018)

del v1.year

print (v1.age)

OUTPUT – 'Vehicle' object has no 'year' attribute

You can also use the "del" keyword to entirely **delete an object**, as shown in the example below:

class Vehicle:

    def __init__ (refobject, name, year)
    refobject.name = name
    refobject.name = year

def newfunc (xyz):

    print ("I am a proud owner of " + xyz.name)

v1 = Vehicle ("AUDI", 2018)

del v1

OUTPUT – NameError: 'v1' is not defined

The "Pass" Statement

The definition of a Python Class must contain values or you will receive an error. However, there might be instances when the definition of a class does not have any content. In such case, you can use the "pass" statement to avoid getting an error. Look at the example below:

```
class Vehicle:          # this class definition is empty
    pass                # used to avoid any errors
```

EXERCISE – Create a Class "KafeShop" with properties as "type" and "size" with corresponding values as "cappuccino" and "large" respectively.

USE YOUR DISCRETION HERE AND WRITE YOUR CODE FIRST

Now, check your code against the correct code below:

```
class KafeShop:
    def __init__ (refobject, type, size)
    refobject.type = type
    refobject.size = size
```

c1 = KafeShop ("cappuccino", "large")

print (c1.type)
print (c1.size)
OUTPUT – cappuccino   *large*

EXERCISE – Create a Class "KafeShop" with properties as "type" and "size" with corresponding values as "cappuccino" and "large" respectively. Create a new function "funct1" that would print "I would like to order a" and execute it on the object.

****USE YOUR DISCRETION HERE AND WRITE YOUR CODE FIRST****

Now, check your code against the correct code below:

class KafeShop:

     def __init__ (refobject, type, size)
     refobject.type = type
     refobject.size = size

     def funct1 (refobject):
     print ("I would like to order a" + refobject.type)

c1 = KafeShop ("cappuccino", "large")

c1.funct1 ( )

OUTPUT – I would like to order a cappuccino

Python Operators

In Python, a variety of Operators can be used to perform operations on a Python variable and its values. The different groups of Python operators are provided below:

Arithmetic Operators can be utilized with numerical values to execute basic math calculations.

Name	Operator	Sample
Add	+	J + K
Subtract	-	J - K
Multiply	*	J * K
Divide	/	J / K
Modulus	%	J % K
Exponentiation	**	J ** K
Floor division	//	J // K

Assignment Operators can be utilized for assignment of values to a variable.

Name	Sample
=	J = 5
+=	J += 3
-=	J -= 3

*=	J *= 3
/=	J /= 3
%=	J %= 3
//=	J //= 3
**=	J **= 3
&=	J &= 3
|=	J |= 3
^=	J ^= 3
>>=	J >>= 3
<<=	J <<= 3

Comparison Operators can be utilized to draw comparison between the values.

Name	Operator	Sample
Equal	==	J == K
Not equal	!=	J != K
Greater than	>	J > K
Less than	<	J < K
Greater than or equal to	>=	J >= K
Less than or equal to	<=	J <= K

Logical Operators can be utilized to generate a combination of conditional statements.

Operator	Usage	Sample
and	Will return "True" if both the statements hold true.	J < 5 and J < 10

| or | Will return "True" if one of the statements holds true. | J < 5 or J < 4 |
| not | Will reverse the results and return "False" if the results are true. | Not (J < 5 and J < 10) |

Identity Operators can be utilized to draw a comparison between two objects to check whether the same object was created more than once using the same memory location.

Operator	Usage	Sample
is	Will return true if the two variables are the same object.	J is K
is not	Will return true if the two variables are not the same object.	J is not K

Membership Operators can be utilized to test if select sequence can be found in an object.

Operator	Usage	Sample
in	Will return True if a sequence with a specific value can be found in the object.	J in K
not in	Will return True if a sequence with a specific value cannot be found in the object.	J not in K

Bitwise Operators can be utilized to draw a comparison between two numeric values.

Oper ator	Usage	Sample
&	AND	Will set each bit to 1 if the two bits are 1
|	OR	Will set each bit to 1 if one of the two bits is 1
^	XOR	Will set each bit to 1 if only one of the two bits is 1
~	NOT	Will invert all the bits
<<	Zero fill left shift	Shifts left by pushing zero in from the right, making the left most bit to be dropped
>>	Signed right shift	Shifts right by pushing copies of the left most bit in from the left, making the right most bit to be dropped

Chapter 5:

Built-In Python Functions

Python Built-In Functions

Like most programming languages, Python boasts a number of built-in functions to make your life easier while coding a software program. Here is a list of all such built-in functions:

Function	Description
abs ()	Will result in the absolute values of the numbers.
all ()	Will result in True if all items within an iterative object are true.
any ()	Will result in True if any item of the iterative object holds true.
ascii ()	Will result in a readable version of an object and replace non-ascii characters with escape characters.
bin ()	Will result in the binary version of the numbers.
bool ()	Will result in the boolean values of indicated objects.
bytearray ()	Will result in an array of bytes.

bytes ()	Will result in bytes objects.
callable ()	Will result in True if a specific object is callable or else results in False.
chr ()	Will result in a character from the indicated Unicode code.
classmethod ()	Will convert any method into class method.
compile ()	Will result in the indicated source as an object, ready for execution.
complex ()	Will result in a complex number.
delattr ()	Will delete specific attributes (property or method) from the indicated object.
dict ()	Will result in a dictionary.
dir ()	Will result in a list of properties and methods of the specific object.
divmod ()	Will result in the quotient and the remainder when one argument is divided by another.
enumerate ()	Will take a collection and result in enumerate objects.
eval ()	Will evaluate and execute an expression.
exec ()	Will execute the indicated code (or object)
filter ()	Uses a filter function to exclude items in an iterative object.
float ()	Will result in floating point numbers.
format ()	Will format the indicated value.
frozenset ()	Will result in a frozen set object.
getattr ()	Will result in the value of the indicated attribute (property or method).
globals ()	Will result in the most recent global symbol table as a dictionary.
hasattr ()	Will result in True if the indicated object has the indicated attribute.
hash ()	Will result in the hash value of the indicated object.
help ()	Will execute the built-in help system.

hex ()	Conversion of numbers into hexadecimal values.
id ()	Will result in the identity of an object.
input ()	Will allow user input.
int ()	Will result in an integer number.
isinstance ()	Will result in True if the indicated object is an instance of the indicated object.
issubclass ()	Will result in True if the indicated class is a subclass of the indicated object.
iter ()	Will result in an iterative object.
len ()	Will result in the length of an object.
list ()	Will result in a list.
locals ()	Will result in an updated dictionary of the current local symbol table.
map ()	Will result in the indicated iterator with the indicated function applied to each item.
max ()	Will result in the largest item of an iteration.
memoryview ()	Will result in memory view objects.
min ()	Will result in the smallest item of an iteration.
next ()	Will result in the next item in an iteration.
object ()	Will result in a new object.
oct ()	Converts a number into an octet.
open ()	Will open files and result in file objects.
ord ()	Conversion of an integer representing the Unicode of the indicated character.
pow ()	Will result in the value of a to the power of b.
print ()	Will print to the standard output device.
property ()	Will retrieve, set, and delete a property.
range ()	Will result in a sequence of numbers, beginning from 0 and default increments of 1.

repr ()	Will result in a readable version of objects.
reversed ()	Will result in a reversed iteration.
round ()	Rounding of a number.
set ()	Will result in new set objects.
setattr ()	Will set attributes of the objects.
slice ()	Will result in a sliced objects.
sorted ()	Will result in sorted lists.
staticmethod ()	Will convert methods into a static method.
str ()	Will result in string objects.
sum ()	Will sum the items of iterations.
super ()	Will result in an object representing the parent class.
tuple ()	Will result in tuples.
type ()	Will result in the type of objects.
vars ()	Will result in the _dict_ property of objects.
zip ()	Will result in a single iteration from multiple iterations.

Python Built-In String Methods

There are a number of built-in Python methods specifically for strings of data, which will result in new values for the string without making any changes to the original string. Here is a list of all such methods.

Method	Description
capitalize ()	Will convert the initial character to upper case.
casefold ()	Will convert strings into lower case.
center ()	Will result in centered strings.
count ()	Will result in the number of times an indicated value appears in a string.

encode ()	Will result in an encoded version of the strings.
endswith ()	Will result in true if the string ends with the indicated value.
expandtabs ()	Will set the tab size of the string.
find ()	Will search the string for indicated value and result in its position.
format ()	Will format indicated values of strings.
format_map ()	Will format indicated values of strings.
index ()	Will search the string for indicated value and result in its position.
isalnum ()	Will result in True if all string characters are alphanumeric.
isalpha ()	Will result in True if all string characters are alphabets.
isdecimal ()	Will result in True if all string characters are decimals.
isdigit ()	Will result in True if all string characters are digits.
isidentifier ()	Will result in True if the strings is an identifier.
islower ()	Will result in True if all string characters are lower case.
isnumeric ()	Will result in True if all string characters are numeric.
isprintable ()	Will result in True if all string characters are printable.
isspace ()	Will result in True if all string characters are whitespaces.
istitle ()	Will result in True if the string follows the rules of a title.
isupper ()	Will result in True if all string characters are upper case.
join ()	Will join the elements of an iteration to the end of the string.

ljust ()	Will result in a left-justified version of the string.
lower ()	Will convert a string into lower case.
lstrip ()	Will result in a left trim version of the string.
maketrans ()	Will result in a translation table to be used in translations.
partition ()	Will result in a tuple where the string is separated into 3 sections.
replace ()	Will result in a string where an indicated value is replaced with another indicated value.
rfind ()	Will search the string for an indicated value and result in its last position.
rindex ()	Will search the string for an indicated value and result in its last position.
rjust ()	Will result in the right justified version of the string.
rpartition ()	Will result in a tuple where the string is separated into 3 sections.
rsplit ()	Will split the string at the indicated separator and result in a list.
rstrip ()	Will result in a new string version that has been trimmed at its right.
split ()	Will split the string at the indicated separator and result in a list.
splitlines ()	Will split the string at line breaks and result in a list.
startswith ()	Will result in true if the string starts with the indicated value.
strip ()	Will result in a trimmed version of the string.
swapcase ()	Will swap the alphabet cases.
title ()	Will convert the first character of each word to upper case.
translate ()	Will result in a translated string.
upper ()	Will convert a string into upper case.

| zfill () | Will fill the string with the indicated number of 0 values at the beginning. |

Python Random Numbers

A "random ()" function does not exist in Python, but it has an embedded module called "random" that may be utilized to create numbers randomly when needed. For instance, if you wanted to call the "random" module and display a number randomly between 100 and 500, you can accomplish this by executing the code below:

```
import random
print (random.randrange (100, 500))
```

OUTPUT – Any number between 100 and 500 will be randomly displayed.

There are a number of defined methods in the random module as listed below:

Method	Description
betavariate ()	Will result in random float numbers between 0 and 1 based on the Beta distribution.
choice ()	Will result in random elements on the basis of the provided sequence.
choices ()	Will result in a list consisting of a random selection from the provided sequence.
expovariate ()	Will result in a float number randomly displayed between 0 and -1, or between 0 and 1 for negative parameters on the basis of the statistical exponential distributions.

gammavariate ()	Will result in a float number displayed between 0 and 1 on the basis of the statistical Gamma distribution.
gauss ()	Will result in a float number displayed between 0 and 1 on the basis of the Gaussian distribution, which is widely utilized in probability theory.
getrandbits ()	Will result in a number that represents the random bits.
getstate ()	Will result in the current internal state of the random number generator.
lognormvariate ()	Will result in a float number randomly displayed between 0 and 1 on the basis of a log-normal distribution, which is widely utilized in probability theory.
normalvariate()	Will result in a float number randomly displayed between 0 and 1 on the basis of the normal distribution, which is widely utilized in probability theory.
paretovariate ()	Will result in a float number randomly displayed between 0 and 1 on the basis of the Pareto distribution, which is widely utilized in probability theory.
randint ()	Will result in a random number between the provided range.
random ()	Will result in a float number randomly displayed between 0 and 1.
randrange ()	Will result in a random number between the provided range.
sample ()	Will result in a sample of the sequences.
seed ()	Will trigger the random number generator.
setstate ()	Will restore the internal state of the random number generator.
shuffle ()	Will take a sequence and result in a sequence but in some random order.
triangular ()	Will result in a random float number between two provided parameters. You

	could also set a mode parameter for specification of the midpoint between the two other parameters.
uniform ()	Will result in a random float number between two provided parameters.
vonmisesvari ate()	Will result in a float number randomly displayed between 0 and 1 on the basis of the von "Mises distribution", which is utilized in directional statistics.
weibullvariat e()	Will result in a float number randomly displayed between 0 and 1 on the basis of the Weibull distribution, which is utilized in statistics.

Python Built-In List Methods

Python supports a number of built-in methods that can be used on lists or arrays, as listed in the table below:

Method	Description
append ()	Will insert an element at the end of the list.
clear ()	Will remove all the list elements.
copy ()	Will result in a replica of the list.
count ()	Will result in the number of elements with the indicated value.
extend ()	Will add the elements of a list (or any iterator), to the end of the current list.
index ()	Will result in the index of the first element with the indicated value.
insert ()	Will add an element at the indicated position.
pop ()	Will remove the element at the indicated position.
remove ()	Will remove the first item with the indicated value.
reverse ()	Will reverse the order of the list.
sort ()	Will sort the list.

Python Built-In Tuple Methods

Python supports a couple of built-in methods that can be used on tuples, as listed in the table below:

Method	Description
count ()	Will result in the number of times an indicated value appears in the tuple.
index ()	Will search a tuple for the indicated value and result in the position of where the value is found.

Python Built-In Set Methods

Python also supports a variety of embedded methods that can be used on sets that are listed in the table below:

Method	Description
"add ()"	Will add an element to the set.
"clear ()"	Will remove all the elements from the set.
"copy ()"	Will result in a replica of the set.
"difference ()"	Will result in a set that contains the difference between 2 or more sets.
"difference_upda te ()"	Will remove the items from a set that can be found in another, indicated set.
"discard ()"	Will remove the indicated item.
"intersection ()"	Will result in a set that is the intersection of couple other sets.
"intersection_up date ()"	Will remove the items from a set that are not present in another indicated set.
"isdisjoint ()"	Will determine if intersection exists between two sets.

"issubset ()"	Will determine if the identified set contains another set.
"issuperset ()"	Will determine if a different set contain the identified set or not.
"pop ()"	Will remove an element from the set.
"remove ()"	Will remove the indicated element.
"symmetric_diffe rence ()"	Will result in a set with the symmetric differences of the two indicated sets.
"symmetric_diffe rence_update ()"	Will insert the symmetric differences from the indicated set and other sets.
"union ()"	Will result in a set containing the union of sets.
"update ()"	Will update the set with the union of the indicated set and other sets.

Python Built-In Dictionary Methods

Python also supports a large number of built-in methods that can be used on dictionaries that are listed in the table below:

Method	Description
clear ()	Will remove all the elements from the dictionary.
copy ()	Will result in a copy of the dictionary.
fromkeys ()	Will result in a dictionary with the indicated keys and values.
get ()	Will result in the values of the indicated key.
items ()	Will result in a list containing a tuple for every key-value pair.
keys ()	Will result in a list containing the keys of the dictionary.
pop ()	Will remove the elements with the indicated key.
popitem ()	Will remove the key value pair that was most recently added.

setdefault ()	Will result in the values of the indicated key. In case the key is not found, a new key will be added with the indicated values.
update ()	Will update the dictionary with the indicated key value pairs.
values ()	Will result in a list of all the values in the dictionary.

Python Built-In File Methods

Python also supports a large number of built-in methods that can be used on file objects that are listed in the table below:

Method	Description
close ()	Will close the file
detach ()	Will result in a separate raw stream.
fileno ()	Will result in a number representing the stream, per the operating system processing.
flush ()	Will flush the internal buffer.
isatty ()	Will result in determination if the file stream is interactive.
read ()	Will result in the content of the file.
readable ()	Will result in determination if the file stream is readable or not.
readline ()	Will result in one line from the file.
readlines ()	Will result in a list of lines from the file.
seek ()	Will modify the position of the file.
seekable ()	Will result in determination if the file permits modification of its position.
tell ()	Will result in the current position of the file.
truncate ()	Will change the size of the file to the indicated value.
writeable ()	Will result in determination if the file permits writing over.
write ()	Will write the indicated string to the file.
writelines ()	Will writes a list of strings to the file.

Python Keywords

Python contains some keywords that cannot be used to define a variable or used as a function name or any other unique identifier. These select Python keywords are listed in the table below:

Method	Description
"and"	Logical operator.
"as"	For creating an alias.
"assert"	To debug.
"break"	For breaking out of a loop.
"class"	For defining a class.
"continue"	For continuing to the next iteration of a loop.
"def"	For defining a function.
"del"	For deleting an object.
"elif"	For use in conditional statements, similar to "else if".
"else"	For use in conditional statements.
"except"	For use with exceptions, so the program knows the steps to follow in case of an exception.
"FALSE"	One of the data values assigned only to Boolean data type.
"finally"	For use with exceptions, this set of code would be executed regardless of any occurrences of an exception.
"for"	Used in creation of a "for loop".
"from"	For importing particular part of a module.
"global"	For declaring a global variable.
"if"	For making conditional statements.
"import"	For importing desired module.

"in"	For checking a specific data value within a tuple or a list.
"is"	For testing two variables that may be equal.
"lambda"	For creating an anonymous function.
"None"	For representation of null data value.
"nonlocal"	For declaration of a non-local variable.
"not"	Logical operator.
"or"	Logical operator.
"pass"	Will result in a null statement that would not be executed.
"raise"	Used to raise an exception to the statement.
"result in"	Used for exiting a function and resulting in a data value.
"TRUE"	One of the data values assigned only to Boolean data type.
"try"	Used for making "try except" statements.
"while"	For creating a "while loop".
"with"	Used for simplification of the handling procedure for exceptions.
"yield"	For terminating a function and resulting in a generator.

Review Quiz

Answer the questions below to verify your understanding of the concepts explained in this chapter. The answer key can be found at the end of the quiz.

1. Name the built-in function that will allow you to output Boolean values of indicated objects.

2. Name the built-in function that will allow you to output a list of properties and methods of the specific object.

3. Name the built-in function that will allow you to output an updated dictionary of the current local symbol table.

4. Name the built-in function that will allow you to define the attributes of the objects.

5. Name the built-in string method that will allow you to convert the initial character to upper case.

6. Name the built-in string method that will allow you to search the string for indicated value and result in its position.

7. Name the built-in string method that will allow you to join the elements of an iteration to the end of the string.

8. Name the built-in string method that will allow you to replace an indicated value of a string into another one.

9. Name the built-in random number method that will allow you to output a list consisting of a random selection from the provided sequence.

10.   Name the built-in random number method that will allow you to output the current internal state of the random number generator.

11. Name the built-in random number method that will allow you to output a float number randomly displayed between 0 and 1.

12. Name the built-in random number method that will allow you to output a random float number between two provided parameters.

13. Name the built-in list method that will allow you to insert an element at the end of the list.

14. Name the built-in list method that will allow you to add the elements of a list (or any iterator), to the end of the current list.

15. Name the built-in tuple method that will allow you to output the number of times an indicated value appears in the tuple.

16. Name the built-in tuple method that will allow you to search a tuple for the indicated value and result in the position of where the value is found.

17. Name the built in Set method that will allow you to remove all the elements from the set.

18. Name the built in Set method that will allow you to output a set that is the intersection of couple other sets.

19. Name the built in Dictionary method that will allow you to output a dictionary with the indicated keys and values.

20. Name the built in Dictionary method that will allow you to remove the key value pair that was most recently added.

Answer Key

1. bool ( )
2. dir ( )
3. locals ( )
4. setattr ( )
5. capitalize ( )
6. find ( )

7. join ( )

8. replace ( )

9. choices ( )

10. getstate ( )

11. random ( )

12. uniform ( )

13. append ( )

14. extend ( )

15. count ( )

16. index ( )

17. clear ( )

18. intersection ( )

19. fromkeys ( )

20. popitem ( )

Chapter 6:

Python Applications

Python is widely used for a large variety of web-based projects spanning across the industrial spectrum. In the last chapter, you learnt about development of websites and web-based applications using a Python based data framework. Python is widely used in development and testing of software programs, machine learning algorithms and Artificial Intelligence technologies to solve real world problems. The science of developing human controlled and operated machinery, such as digital computers or robots, that can mimic human intelligence, adapt to new inputs and perform human like tasks is called "Artificial Intelligence" or AI. Let's look at real life applications of the Python programming language in different arenas of the modern life. Some of the widely used web frameworks such as "Django" and "Flask" have been developed using Python. These frameworks assist the developer in writing server-side codes that enable management of database, generation of backend programming logic, mapping of URL, among others.

A variety of machine learning models have been written exclusively in Python. Machine learning is a way for machines to write logic in order to learn and fix a specific issue on its own. For instance, Python-based machine learning algorithms used in development of "product recommendation systems" for eCommerce businesses such as Amazon, Netflix, YouTube and many more. Other instances of Python based machine learning models are the facial recognition and the voice recognition technologies available on our mobile devices. Python can also be used in the development of data visualization and data analysis tools and techniques such as scatter plots and other graphical representations of data. "Scripting" can be defined as the process of generating simple programs for automation of straightforward tasks like those required to send automated email responses and text messages. You could develop these types of software using the Python programming language. A wide variety of gaming programs have been developed with the use of Python. Python also supports the development of "embedded applications." You could use data libraries such as "TKinter" or "QT" to create desktop apps based on Python.

Gaming Industry

Python based artificial intelligence programs are at the heart of the gaming industry with its groundbreaking simulation and virtual experience technologies. In 1949, mathematician Claude Shannon developed a 'one player chess game' using the rudimentary Machine learning algorithms, where people would compete against a computer instead of another person. In 1989, the "Sim City" game successfully stimulated realistic and deeply human characteristics like unpredictability, with its use of artificial intelligence technology. In 2000, the "Total War" game incorporated human like emotions into their virtual fighters mimicking the soldiers in real-life battlefields.

In 2017, the leading gaming company, Electronic Arts, announced establishment of their new research and development division called "SEED". This division is dedicated solely to exploration of artificial intelligence-based technologies and creative opportunities for future giving products. Another billion-dollar gaming company called Epic Games collaborated with CubicMotion, 3Lateral, Tencent, and Vicon to develop in realistic virtual human named "Siren" marking a tremendous step forward in gaming as well as film industry.

Cost Saving

Since the early 1980s, procedural content generation has become an area of grave importance for game development. This pertains to generation of game levels and rules, quest and stories, spatial maps, Music and props such as vehicles, weapons and powers as well as Game characters. This is gaming content creation it's traditionally done by highly skilled Game artists and developers that tend to be expensive and in high demand. Development of a single game requires hundreds of people working for several years adding to the high cost of game development. Consequently, the gaming industry is enticed by the lucrative artificial intelligence technology to create high-quality gaming content at a faction of cost.

In 2018, Nivdia collaborated with an independent game development company called Remedy Entertainment to develop an automated real-time deep learning Technology that can create three-dimensional facial animations from audio. This technology will be useful in development of low-cost localization, in-game dialogue and virtual reality avatars. In 2019, Italy's Politecnico di Milano launched a game level-design artificial intelligence using generative adversarial networks (GANs), which is a deep neutral network composed of two nets contested within each other. A popular first-person shooter video game called "DOOM" now contains maps designed using this technology.

Enhancing Gaming Experience

The gaming industry is leveraging artificial intelligence Technology to understand what players do and how they feel during the play in order to be able to model a human player. To gauge and build models of player experience, supervised machine learning Technologies such as "Artificial Neural Networks" and "Support Vector Machines" are used. Select aspects of the game and player-game interaction serves as the training data resources. For example, the video game "Grand Theft Auto" is being used and the development off autonomous vehicles by training them to recognize stop signs. Another example of gaming technology being leveraged by AI researchers to aid in machine learning is the sandbox video game "Minecraft", which enables players to construct a virtual 3-D world using a variety of building blocks.

Automation and Personalization of Customer Service with Chatbots

With the advancements in the natural language processing technology, the consumers' ability to distinguish between the human voice and the voice of a robot is increasingly diminishing. Chatbots with their more human like voices and ability to resolve customer issues independently and in the absence of human assistance is the future of customer service and it's bound to expand from banking to all other industries. The banks will soon be reporting huge savings and significant cost reductions in the next 10 years. A recent study predicted up to $450 billion in savings by the banking and lending industry by 2030.

Despite this huge promise and reward brought on by AI powered Chatbots, banking and other industries need to tread with caution when it comes to delivering service that meets or succeeds customer expectations. The reality is humans today and for the foreseeable future like to speak with another person to address and resolve their issues. The nuances of human problems seem too far-fetched to be understood by a callus robot. The best approach seems to be human customer service representatives augmented by the Chatbots rather than replacing humans completely. For example, the renowned Swiss bank UBS, with a global ranking of 35 for the volume of its assets, has partnered with Amazon. Amazon has successfully incorporated a "Ask UBS" service on their AI powered speakers called Amazon Echo (Alexa). UBS customers across the world can simply "ask" Alexa for advice and analysis on global financial markets in lieu of The Wall Street Journal. The "Ask UBS" service is also designed to offer definitions and examples for the finance related jargon and acronyms. However, "Ask UBS" application is unable to offer personalized advice to the UBS clients, owing to a lack of access to individual portfolios and client's holding and goals. This inability stems from security and privacy concerns regarding client data.

With the wealth of customer data including records of online and offline transactions and detailed demographics, banking industry is sitting on a gold mine that needs the power of AI based analytics to dig out the gold with data mining. Integration and analysis of information sourced from discrete databases has uniquely positioned banks to utilize Machine learning and obtain a complete view of their customers' needs and provide superior personalized services.

"The next step within the digital service model is for banks to price for the individual, and to negotiate that price in real time, taking personalization to the ultimate level."
– James Eardley, SAP Marketing Director

For all the financial institutions, customer personalization has transcended from marketing and product customization into the realm of cybersecurity. Biometric data, like fingerprints, is increasingly being used to augment or replace traditional passwords and other means of identity verification. A recent study by "Google Intelligence", reported that by 2021 about 2 billion bank customers will be using some or other form of biometric identification. One of the leading tech giants, Apple, has descended onto payment platform and is now using their

Artificial Intelligence powered "facial recognition technology" to unlock their devices and also to validate payments, using their "digital wallet" service called "Apple Pay".

Healthcare Applications

- **AI-assisted robotic surgery** – The biggest draw of robot assisted surgery is that they do not require large incisions and are considered minimally invasive with low post-op recovery time. Robots are capable of analyzing data from pre-op patient medical records and subsequently guiding the surgeon's instruments during surgery. These robot-assisted surgeries have reported up to 21% reduction in patients' hospital stays. Robots can also use data from past surgeries and use AI to inform the surgeon about any new possible techniques. The most advanced surgical robot, "Da Vinci", allows surgeons to carry out complex surgical procedures with higher accuracy and greater control than the conventional methods.

- **Supplement clinical diagnosis** – Although the use of AI in diagnostics is still under the radar, a lot of successful use cases have already been reported. An algorithm created at Stanford University is capable of detecting skin cancer with similar competencies as that of a skilled dermatologist. An AI software program in

Denmark was used to eavesdrop on emergency phone calls made to human dispatchers. The underlying algorithm analyzed the tone and words of the caller as well as the background noise to detect cases of heart attack. The AI program had 93% success rate which was 20% higher than the human counterparts.

- **Virtual Nursing Assistants** – The virtual nurses are available 24*7 without fatigue and lapse in judgment. They provide constant patient monitoring and directions for the most effective care while answering all of the patient's questions quickly and efficiently. An increase in regular communication between patients and their care providers can be credited to virtual nursing applications. This prevents unnecessary hospital visits and readmission. The virtual nurse assistant at Care Angel can already provide wellness checks through Artificial Intelligence and voice.

- **Automation of administrative tasks** – AI driven technology such as voice to text transcriptions are aiding in ordering test, prescribing medications and even writing medical chart notes. The partnership between IBM and Cleveland Clinic has allowed IBM's Watson to perform mining on clinical health data and help physicians in developing personalized and more efficient treatment plans.

Transportation Industry

The transportation industry is highly susceptible two problems arising from human errors, traffic and for accidents. These problems are too difficult to model owing to their inherently unpredictable nature but can be easily overcome with the use of Artificial Intelligence powered tools that can analyze observed data and make or predict the appropriate decisions. The challenge of increasing travel demand, safety concerns, CO2 emissions and environmental degradation can be met with the power of artificial intelligence. From Artificial Neural Networks to Bee colony optimization, a whole lot of artificial intelligence techniques are being employed to make transportation industry efficient and effective. To obtain significant relief from traffic congestion while making travel time more reliable for the population, transport authorities are experimenting with a variety of AI based solutions. With potential application of artificial intelligence for enhanced road infrastructure and assistance for drivers, transportation industry it's focused on accomplishing a more reliable transport system, which will have limited to no effect on the environment while being cost effective.

It is an uphill battle to fully understand the relationships between the characteristics of various transportation systems using the traditional methods. Artificial intelligence is here once again to offer the panacea by transforming the traffic sensors on the road into a smart agent that can potentially detect accidents and predict the future traffic conditions. Rapid development has been observed in the area of Intelligent Transport Systems (ITS), which are targeted to alleviate traffic congestion and improve driving experience by utilizing multiple Technologies and communication systems. They are capable of collecting and storing data that can be easily integrated with machine learning technology. To increase the efficiency of police patrol and keeping the citizens of safe collection of crime data is critical and can be achieved with right AI powered tools. Artificial intelligence can also simplify the transportation planning of the road freight transport system, by providing accurate prediction methods to forecast their volume.

Here are some real-world examples of artificial intelligence being used in the transportation industry:

- Local motors company in collaboration with IBM's Watson has unveiled an AI powered autonomous fully electric vehicle called "Olli".

- A highly promising traffic control system developed by Rapid Flow Technologies is called "SURTRAC", which allows traffic lights at intersections to respond to vehicular flow on an individual level instead of being a part of a centralized system.

- A Chinese company called "TuSimple" entered American market with their self-driving trucks that can utilize long distance sensors with a complete observation range and it's deep learning artificial intelligence technology allows seamless detection and tracking of objects using multiple cameras.

- Rolls-Royce is expected to launch air own clueless cargo ships by 2020 that could be controlled remotely and pioneer the way for fully autonomous ships in near future.

- In early 2019, the first autonomous trains were tested by the London underground train system that can potentially carry more passengers in lieu of driver's cabin.

- Some commuters in Sweden have reportedly been testing microchip implants on their body as travel tickets.

- China launched the Autonomous Rail Rapid Transit System (ART) in the city of Zhuzhou that doesn't require tracks and instead, the trains follow of virtual track created by painted dashed lines.

- Autonomous delivery trucks could soon be bringing our food and mail to us instead of the human driven delivery service.

- Dubai is experimenting with Smart technology driven digital number plates for cars, which can immediately send an alert to the authorities in the event of an accident.

- Some of the American airports are you using artificial intelligence a face scanning technologies to verify the identities of passengers before allowing them to board the flight and ditching the traditional passports.

- The revolutionizing Google flights technology is able to predict flight delays before the airlines themselves by using Advanced machine learning technology on the available data from previous flights and providing passengers a more accurate expected time of arrival.

- When it comes to real-time customer service, the Trainline app has surpassed all AI powered applications on the market, with its BusyBot technology that can help the passengers with their change tickets booking and purchase as well as find a vacant seat on the train in real-time. This bot collects information from the passengers onboard on how busy their carriages are and then analyzes that data to advise other passengers on potentially vacant seating.

- The "JOZU" app is aimed at once again liberating the modern woman who likes to travel alone and is concerned about her safety. It collects user data to provide women with the safest routes and methods of transport.

- China has pioneered the development of smart highway that can charge electric vehicles as they are driving and Australia is set to follow the lead. Smart roads are being designed to incorporate sensors to monitor traffic patterns and solar panels for vehicle charging.

- Smart luggage with built-in GPS tracker and weighing scales connected to your phones are already available on the market.

- Ford has recently announced its plan to file a patent for their Artificial Intelligence based unmanned "Robotic Police Car" that can issue tickets for speeding and other violations to drivers by scanning their car registration and accessing the CCTV footage.

- Japan will soon be enjoying a new ride-hailing service. Sony recently announced launch of their new service that will use Artificial Intelligence to manage fleets and provide an overview of potential traffic issues like congestions and detours due to public events.

- Ford has designed a "Smart City" with the system that allows smart vehicles to connect and coordinate with one another while cutting down on the risks of collisions and other accidents. The Smart city would collect data from its residents and share it with multiple smart technologies working in tandem to create a digital utopia.

Python Tips and Tricks for Developers

Here are some of the tips and tricks you can leverage to sharpen up your Python programming skill set are:

In-place swapping of two numbers:

```
x, y = 102, 202
print (x, y)
x, y = y, x
print (x, y)"
```

Resulting Output =
102 202
202 102

Reversing a string:

```
x = "christmas"
```

print ("Reverse is", x [::-1])

Resulting Output =
Reverse is samtsirhc.

Creating a single string from multiple list elements:
x = ["have", "a", "happy","new", "year"]
print (" ".join (x))

Resulting Output =
have a happy new year

Stacking of comparison operators:
n = 102
result = 1 < n < 202
print (result)
result = 1 > n <= 92
print (result)

Resulting Output =
True
False

Print the file path of the imported modules:
import os;
import socket;

print(os)
print (socket

Resulting Output =
"<module 'os' from '/usr/lib/python3.5/os.py'>
<module 'socket' from '/usr/lib/python3.5/socket.py'>"

Use of enums in Python:
class MyName:
*   Eye, For, Eye= range (3)*

print (MyName.Eye)

print (MyName.For)
print (MyName.Eye)

Resulting Output =
2
1
2

Result in multiple values from functions:
def x ():
*   result in 12, 22, 32, 42*
a, b, c, d = x ()

print (a, b, c, d)

Resulting Output =
12 22 32 42

Identify the value with highest frequency:
test = [11, 21, 31, 41, 21, 21, 31, 11, 41, 41, 41]
print (max(set(test), key = test.count))

Resulting Output =
41

Check the memory usage of an object:
import sys
x = 1
print (sys.getsizeof (x))

Resulting Output =
28

Printing a string N times:
n = 3;
a ="PythonCoding";
*print (a * n);*

Resulting Output =

PythonCodingPythonCodingPythonCoding

Identify anagrams:
from collections import Counter
def is_anagram (str1, str2):
*   result in Counter(str1) == Counter(str2)*
print (is_anagram ('home', 'emoh'))

print (is_anagram ('home', 'rome'))

Resulting Output =
True
False

Transposing a matrix:
mat = [[12, 22, 32], [42, 52, 62]]
*zip (*mat)*

Resulting Output =
[(12, 42), (22, 52), (32, 62)]

Print a repeated string without using loops:
*print "Python"*3+' '+"Programming"*2*

Resulting Output =
PythonPythonPython ProgrammingProgramming

Measure the code execution time:
import time
startTime = time.time()
"write your code or functions calls"
"write your code or functions calls"

endTime = time.time ()
totalTime = endTime – startTime
print ('Total time required to execute code is=' , totalTime)

Resulting Output =
Total time

Obtain the difference between two lists:
list1 = ['Ryan', 'Prim', 'Keith', 'Dan', 'Sam']
list2 = ['Sam', 'Dan', 'Keith']
set1 = set(list1)
set2 = set(list2)
list3 = list(set1.symmetric_difference(set2))
print(list3)

Resulting Output =
list3 = ['Ryan', 'Prim']

Calculate the memory being used by an object in Python:
import sys
list1 = ['Ryan', 'Prim', 'Keith', 'Dan', 'Sam']
print ("size of list = ", sys.getsizeof(list1))
name = 'pynative.com'
print ('size of name =', sys.getsizeof(name))

Resulting Output =
('size of list = ', 112)
('size of name = ', 49)

Removing duplicate items from the list:
listNumbers = [40, 44, 44, 46, 48, 48, 40, 30, 44]
print ('Original=' , listNumbers)
listNumbers = list(set(listNumbers))
print ('After removing duplicate= ' , listNumbers)

Resulting Output =
'Original= ', [40, 44, 44, 46, 48, 48, 40, 30, 44]
'After removing duplicate= ', [40, 44, 44, 46, 48, 30]

Find if a list contains identical elements:
listOne = [18, 18, 18, 18]
print ('All elements are duplicate in listOne',
listOne.count(listOne[0]) == len(listOne))

listTwo = [18, 18, 18, 50]

print ('All elements are duplicate in listTwo',
listTwo.count(listTwo[0]) == len(listTwo))

Resulting Output =
"'All elements are duplicate in listOne', True"
"'All elements are duplicate in listTwo', False"

Efficiently compare two unordered lists:
from collections import Counter
one = [33, 22, 11, 44, 55]
two = [22, 11, 44, 55, 33]
print ('is two list are b equal', Counter(one) ==
Counter(two))

Resulting Output =
"'is two list are b equal', True"

Check if list contains all unique elements:
def isUnique(item):
tempSet = set ()
result in not any (i in tempSet or tempSet.add(i) for i in
item)
listOne = [123, 345, 456, 23, 567]
print ('All List elements are Unique' , isUnique(listOne))
listTwo = [123, 345, 567, 23, 567]
print ('All List elements are Unique' , isUnique(listTwo))

Resulting Output =
"All List elements are Unique True"
"All List elements are Unique False"

Convert Byte into String:
byteVar = b"pynative"
str = str (byteVar.decode ('utf-8'))
print ('Byte to string is', str)

Resulting Output =
"Byte to string is pynative"

Merge two dictionaries into a single expression:
currentEmployee = {1: 'Scott', 2: 'Eric', 3:'Kelly'}
formerEmployee = {2: 'Eric', 4: 'Emma'}
def merge_dicts(dictOne, dictTwo):
dictThree = dictOne.copy()
dictThree.update(dictTwo)
result in dictThree
print (merge_dicts (currentEmployee, formerEmployee))

Conclusion

Thank you for making it through to the end of Think Python: *A beginner's guide with machine programming language, including an intensive course with step-by-step exercises to learn Python code in 7 days*, let's hope it was informative and able to provide you with all of the tools you need to achieve your goals whatever they may be.

The next step is to utilize your python programming skills and develop new tools and programs to solve real world problems. Python programming language has rendered itself as the language of choice for coding beginners and advanced software programmers alike. This book is written to help you master the basic concepts of Python coding and how you can utilize your coding skills to analyze a large volume of data and uncover valuable information that can otherwise be easily lost in the volume. Python was designed primarily to emphasize readability of the programming code, and its syntax enables programmers to convey ideas using fewer lines of code. Python programming language increases the speed of operation while allowing for higher efficiency in creating system integrations.. The power of programming languages in our digital world cannot be underestimated. People are increasingly reliable on the modern conveniences of the smart technology and that momentum will endure for a long time. With all the instructions provided in this book, you are now ready to start developing your own innovative smart tech ideas and turn it into major tech startup company and guide the mankind towards a smarter future.

Finally, if you found this book useful in any way, a review on Amazon is always appreciated!